TERRORISM, HOT SPOTS AND CONFLICT-RELATED ISSUES

AUTHORIZATION FOR USE OF MILITARY FORCE AGAINST THE ISLAMIC STATE

ISSUES AND PROPOSALS

TERRORISM, HOT SPOTS AND CONFLICT-RELATED ISSUES

Additional books in this series can be found on Nova's website under the Series tab.

Additional e-books in this series can be found on Nova's website under the e-book tab.

TERRORISM, HOT SPOTS AND CONFLICT-RELATED ISSUES

AUTHORIZATION FOR USE OF MILITARY FORCE AGAINST THE ISLAMIC STATE

ISSUES AND PROPOSALS

TOMAS MENDOZA
EDITOR

nova publishers
New York

Library of Congress Cataloging-in-Publication Data

ISBN: 978-1-63483-556-5

Published by Nova Science Publishers, Inc. † New York

CONTENTS

Preface		**vii**
Chapter 1	A New Authorization for Use of Military Force Against the Islamic State: Issues and Current Proposals in Brief *Matthew C. Weed*	**1**
Chapter 2	2001 Authorization for Use of Military Force: Issues Concerning Its Continued Application *Matthew C. Weed*	**37**
Chapter 3	The "Islamic State" Crisis and U.S. Policy *Christopher M. Blanchard, Carla E. Humud, Kenneth Katzman and Matthew C. Weed*	**61**
Index		**119**

PREFACE

In 2014, the armed offensive of the Islamic State (IS, also known as ISIL, ISIS, or Daesh) in northern and western Iraq and northeastern Syria raised significant concerns for the United States. After first ordering multiple deployments of U.S. troops to Iraq to provide security to diplomatic personnel and facilities, advise Iraqi security forces, and conduct intelligence gathering and reconnaissance, President Obama began ordering U.S. military airstrikes on IS forces in Iraq in August 2014. Later in September, after laying out plans for expanded use of military force against the Islamic State in a televised speech to the American people, the President ordered U.S. military airstrikes in Syria against both IS forces and forces of the "Khorasan Group," identified by the President as part of Al Qaeda. The intensified U.S. military engagement has raised numerous questions in Congress and beyond about the President's authority to use military force against the Islamic State. This book discusses the issues and current proposals for the use of military force against the Islamic State.

In: Authorization for Use of Military Force ... ISBN: : 978-1-63483-556-5
Editor: Tomas Mendoza

Chapter 1

A NEW AUTHORIZATION FOR USE OF MILITARY FORCE AGAINST THE ISLAMIC STATE: ISSUES AND CURRENT PROPOSALS IN BRIEF*

Matthew C. Weed

THE IS CRISIS AND THE U.S. RESPONSE

In 2014, the armed offensive of the Islamic State (IS, also known as ISIL, ISIS, or Daesh) in northern and western Iraq and northeastern Syria raised significant concerns for the United States. After first ordering multiple deployments of U.S. troops to Iraq to provide security to diplomatic personnel and facilities, advise Iraqi security forces, and conduct intelligence gathering and reconnaissance, President Obama began ordering U.S. military airstrikes on IS forces in Iraq in August 2014. Later in September, after laying out plans for expanded use of military force against the Islamic State in a televised speech to the American people, the President ordered U.S. military airstrikes in Syria against both IS forces and forces of the "Khorasan Group," identified by the President as part of Al Qaeda. The intensified U.S. military engagement has raised numerous questions in Congress and beyond about the President's

* This is an edited, reformatted and augmented version of a Congressional Research Service publication R43760, prepared for Members and Committees of Congress dated February 20, 2015.

authority to use military force against the Islamic State.[1] Efforts began near the end of the 113th Congress to consider enactment of a new authorization for use of military force targeting the Islamic State, and have continued into the 114th Congress. In addition, the President provided Congress a new authorization proposal in February 2015.

PRESIDENTIAL AUTHORITY TO USE MILITARY FORCE AGAINST THE ISLAMIC STATE

The President in his August 2014 notifications to Congress of deployments and airstrikes in Iraq indicated his powers as Commander in Chief and Chief Executive under Article II of the Constitution gave him authority to undertake such action. Obama Administration officials and the President's September 2014 notifications[2] to Congress for airstrikes and other actions in Iraq and Syria, however, stated that two enacted authorizations for use of military force (AUMFs), the Authorization for Use of Military Force (2001 AUMF; P.L. 107-40), and the Authorization for Use of Military Force Against Iraq Resolution of 2002 (2002 AUMF; P.L. 107-243), provide authorization for certain U.S. military strikes against the Islamic State in Iraq and Syria, as well as the Khorasan Group of Al Qaeda in Syria. After these notifications, however, the President indicated on November 5, 2014, that he intended to enter into discussions with congressional leaders to develop a new AUMF specifically targeting the Islamic State, in order to "right-size and update whatever authorization Congress provides to suit the current fight, rather than previous fights" authorized by the 2001 and 2002 AUMFs.[3] The President called on Congress to enact a new AUMF targeting the Islamic State in his January 2015 State of the Union address, and transmitted a draft AUMF to Congress on February 11, 2015. Both houses are expected to take up consideration of a new AUMF in the near term.

2001 Post-9/11 Authorization for Use of Military Force

In response to the 9/11 terrorist attacks, Congress enacted the AUMF authorizing the President to use military force against "those nations, organizations, or persons he determines planned, authorized, committed, or aided the terrorist attacks that occurred on September 11, 2001, or harbored such organizations or persons.... " Although the Islamic State does not appear to fall within that language, it is possible that the executive branch regards it as one of the "associated forces" fighting alongside Al Qaeda and the Taliban that it asserts are also targetable under the 2001 AUMF.[4] The Obama Administration had stated previous to the latest action against the Islamic State and the Khorasan Group that it will use force against such associated forces under the 2001 AUMF only when they are lawful military targets that "pose a continuing, imminent threat to U.S. persons.... " Due to Al Qaeda's February 2014 disavowal of any remaining ties with the Islamic State, some question whether the Islamic State can be considered an associated force under the 2001 AUMF. The Obama Administration has stated that the Islamic State can be targeted under the 2001 AUMF because its predecessor organization, Al Qaeda in Iraq, communicated and coordinated with Al Qaeda; the Islamic State currently has ties with Al Qaeda fighter and operatives; the Islamic State employs tactics similar to Al Qaeda; and the Islamic State, with its intentions of creating a new Islamic caliphate, is the "true inheritor of Osama bin Laden's legacy."[5]

2002 Authorization for Use of Military Force Against Iraq

Congress enacted the 2002 AUMF prior to the 2003 U.S. invasion of Iraq that toppled the government of Saddam Hussein, with U.S. military deployments to and operations in Iraq continuing until December 2011. The 2002 AUMF authorizes the President to use U.S. Armed Forces to enforce relevant United Nations Security Council resolutions and to "defend the national security of the United States against the continuing threat posed by Iraq.... " Although the 2002 AUMF has no sunset provision and Congress has not repealed it, one view is that after the establishment of a new Iraqi government, the restoration of full Iraqi sovereignty, and the U.S. withdrawal from Iraq, the 2002 AUMF no longer has force. Obama Administration officials have recently voiced support for repealing the 2002 AUMF, reflecting the Administration's belief that it is no longer needed. Conversely, another view asserts that, although its preamble focuses on the Saddam Hussein regime and its WMD programs, the 2002 AUMF's authorization language is broad, referring only to a "continuing threat" from Iraq, and that the 2002 AUMF could provide authority to defend against threats to Iraq as well as threats posed by Iraq. Indeed, 2002 AUMF authority was the basis for the U.S. military presence in Iraq from the fall of Saddam Hussein and completion of the WMD search to its 2011 withdrawal, a span of over eight years, a period that could be characterized as dealing with threats to Iraq rather than threats from Iraq. The IS threat in Iraq could therefore be seen as breathing new life into 2002 AUMF authority. In addition, former supporters of Saddam Hussein reportedly provide support to the Islamic State, possibly forming a link between the original aims of the 2002 AUMF and any future actions taken against the Islamic State.

Presidential Authority Under Article II of the Constitution

Article II of the Constitution makes the President Commander in Chief of the U.S. Armed Forces, and gives the President certain foreign affairs powers. It is debated to what extent Article II authorizes the President to unilaterally use military force, especially given Congress's Article I war powers, including the power to declare war. The President's authority to use force to defend the United States, its personnel, and citizens against ongoing or imminent attack has been generally accepted, while employing such force simply to further foreign policy or general national security goals is more controversial. In Iraq, the President would seem to have substantial authority to use force to defend U.S. personnel, the U.S. embassy in Baghdad, and any other U.S. facilities and property. His August 2014 notifications of airstrikes in Iraq, however, have also cited as justification furthering U.S. national security and foreign policy interests, and have described uses of force to provide humanitarian assistance, and to aid Iraqi security forces in their fight against the Islamic State. In addition, the President's stated strategy for degrading and destroying the Islamic State, as well as his September 2014 notifications to Congress of airstrikes and other actions in Iraq and Syria, are not based primarily on immediate protection of the United States, its personnel, or citizens. Thus, it can be argued that Article II alone might not provide sufficient authorization for the use of military force against IS and Khorasan Group forces in Iraq and Syria.

CALLS FOR A NEW AUMF AND CONGRESSIONAL ACTION IN THE 113TH CONGRESS

Although the Obama Administration has claimed 2001 AUMF and 2002 AUMF authority for its recent and future actions against the Islamic State, these claims have been subject to debate. Some contend that the Administration's actions against the IS also fall outside the President's Article II powers. Concerned with Congress's constitutional role in the exercise of the war power, perceived presidential overreach in that area of constitutional powers, and the President's expansion of the use of military force in Iraq and Syria, several Members of Congress have expressed the view that continued use of military force against the Islamic State requires congressional authorization. Members have differed on whether such authorization is needed, given existing authorities, or whether such a measure should be enacted.

Near the end of the 113th Congress, a number of Members proposed new authorization proposals (several of these are examined in greater detail in the *Appendix*). In December 2014, the Senate Foreign Relations Committee conducted a hearing and considered an IS AUMF proposed by Committee Chairman Robert Menendez. Prior to the committee's markup of the proposal on December 11, the committee held a hearing on December 9 with Secretary of State John Kerry to discuss the Obama Administration's views on enactment of a new IS AUMF. Senator Menendez's IS AUMF proposal, as amended and reported favorably out of committee on December 13 (S.J.Res. 47), would have authorized the use of U.S. Armed Forces against the Islamic State and "associated persons or forces," prohibited "ground combat operations" with limited exceptions, repealed the 2002 AUMF, and sunset the authorization in the 2001 AUMF and the IS AUMF itself three years after enactment.

At the hearing, Secretary Kerry reiterated President Obama's earlier-stated position that the Administration supported enactment of a new AUMF targeting the Islamic State. The Secretary stated that the Administration agreed with the three-year sunset of the authorization contained in Senator Menendez's proposal, "subject to provisions for extension" of that authorization. He stated the Administration's view, however, that such authority "should give the President the clear mandate and flexibility he needs to successfully prosecute the armed conflict against [the Islamic State]," and thus the Administration opposed limitation on the use of ground combat forces, and geographic restriction limiting operations to Iraq and Syria.[6]

The 113th Congress did not ultimately enact a new IS authorization bill, and many Members called upon the President to submit his own proposal. For a comparison of multiple IS AUMFs proposed in the 113th Congress and issues raised by their provisions, see the *Appendix*.

IS AUMF-Related Proposals in the 114TH Congress

Since the start of the 114th Congress, several new proposals for a new IS AUMF or repeal of existing AUMFs have been introduced and others are reportedly being drafted.

On February 2, 2015, Representative Adam Schiff introduced the Authorization for Use of Military Force Against ISIL Resolution (H.J.Res. 27). Pursuant to this proposal, the President would be authorized to use U.S. Armed Forces against the Islamic State, but limited solely to operations in Iraq and Syria, except for U.S. Armed Forces "engaged in training of indigenous Syrian or regional military forces for the purpose of combating" the Islamic State. The resolution states that the authorization does not include "deployment of ground forces in a combat role," except "special operations forces or other forces that may be deployed in a training, advisory, or intelligence capacity." The resolution would terminate the new authority provided by the resolution, as well as repeal the 2001 AUMF, three years after the resolution's enactment. The proposed resolution would repeal the 2002 AUMF immediately upon enactment.

On February 10, 2015, Representative Barbara Lee introduced the Comprehensive Solution to ISIL Resolution (H.J.Res. 30), which does not include a new authorization for the use of military force, but would repeal the 2001 and 2002 AUMFs and place new requirements on the President concerning the campaign against the Islamic State. Repeal of the 2001 and 2002 AUMFs would become effective 60 days after enactment. The proposal states that the policy of the United States is to work through the United Nations and to carry out relevant U.N. Security Council resolutions, support regional efforts to counter the Islamic State, and to ensure U.S. foreign assistance is provided only to Iraqi and Syrian groups subjected to human rights vetting. It requires the President to develop a comprehensive strategy, including strategy for non-military activities, to "degrade and dismantle the Islamic State in Iraq and the Levant (ISIL) and submit to Congress a report that contains the strategy." The President would be required to update the report every 90 days.

Representative Adam Kinzinger introduced the Authorization for Use of Military Force against the Islamic State of Iraq and the Levant (H.J.Res. 33) on February 13, 2015. The proposal would authorize the President "to use the Armed Forces of the United States as the President determines to be necessary and appropriate against the Islamic State of Iraq and the Levant ('ISIL') or associated persons or forces.... " The proposal defines the term "associated persons or forces" as "individuals and organizations fighting for, on behalf of, or alongside ISIL or any closely-related successor entity in hostilities against the United States or its coalition partners."[7] It requires the President to report on activities undertaken pursuant to the authorization every three months, and it would repeal the 2002 AUMF.

Senator Ben Cardin introduced Sunset of the 2001 Authorization for Use of Military Force Act (S. 526) on February 12, 2015. The bill would repeal the 2001 AUMF three years upon enactment.

THE PRESIDENT'S FEBRUARY 2015 IS AUMF PROPOSAL

On February 11, 2015, the President provided Congress with a draft proposal for a new IS AUMF,[8] stating in an accompanying letter that he "can think of no better way for the Congress to join [the President] in supporting our Nation's security than by enacting this legislation, which would show the world we are united in our resolve to counter the threat posed by ISIL."[9] The President's proposal would authorize the use of U.S. Armed Forces that he deems "necessary and appropriate" against the Islamic State and associated persons or forces. In the proposed authorization, "the term 'associated persons or forces' means individuals and organizations fighting for, on behalf of, or alongside ISIL or any closely-related successor entity in hostilities against the United States or its coalition partners." The authorization does not include authority for the use of U.S. Armed Forces for "enduring offensive ground combat operations." The proposal's authorization would terminate three years after enactment, and contains a provision repealing the 2002 AUMF upon enactment. The President would be required to report to Congress at least every six months on actions taken under the proposed IS AUMF.

A number of aspects of the President's proposal could be considered and debated among Members of Congress.

- First, the President's proposal would prohibit "enduring offensive ground combat operations," instead of specifically prohibiting the use of ground combat forces, or execution of ground combat operations, with exceptions for certain types of units or operations, as some of the previous IS AUMF proposals have. It is not clear what that limitation, expressed as it is, would mean in practice, although the President's letter states that it is designed to allow the same excepted units and/or operations.
- Second, the President's proposal does not include any geographical limitation, possibly enabling the use of military force in countries other than Iraq and Syria.
- Third, the definition of "associated persons or forces," especially the inclusion of the phrase "fighting ... on behalf of ... ISIL," might be considered lacking in precision, leading to confusion in the future interpretation of what constitutes a lawfully targeted entity.
- Fourth, the President's proposal, unlike many of the previous IS AUMF proposals, does not provide a purpose or objective for the use of U.S. Armed Forces against the Islamic State in the authorization language itself. This could lead to concerns that the authorization does not sufficiently direct the President's actions or provide a definition of victory, and therefore authorizes military operations without an endpoint or measurable goal.
- Fifth, although the President states in his letter that he still intends to engage Congress in reforming the 2001 AUMF, his proposal does not contain a provision that repeals or sunsets that measure, unlike most of the IS AUMF proposals previously introduced.
- Finally, the reporting requirement is for a basic periodic "actions taken" report, and is similar to certain reporting requirements already in place concerning deployed U.S. Armed Forces. This is in contrast to other IS AUMF proposals, which have required information concerning all targeted entities, specific reports on operations and effectiveness of those operations, and the budget effects of operations.

TYPES OF PROPOSED AUMF PROVISIONS AND RELATED ISSUES

In general, language in a new AUMF targeting the Islamic State and other groups (IS AUMF) could either broaden the purpose of military force to include unspecified U.S. national security interests, or narrow the scope of authorization to specific objectives related to the Administration's stated goal of "degrading and ultimately destroying" the Islamic State. Congress could limit the IS AUMF's geographic scope, authorizing force only in Iraq and/or Syria. With continued uncertainty surrounding the Iraqi government, Congress might include authorization to use U.S. Armed Forces in Iraq in furtherance of political stability objectives. Provisions in any IS AUMF targeting the Islamic State might address the possible effect that targeting the Islamic State in Syria and Iraq could have on the ongoing conflict in Syria. Congress might also include a prohibition on the use of appropriated funds for the use of military force outside the scope of the specified authorization. Proposals for a new IS AUMF might contain provisions to limit presidential authority to use military force against the Islamic State as to scope and duration, and in some cases to sunset or repeal the existing authority in the 2001 and 2002 AUMFs.

The President has stated that an IS authorization should provide the flexibility to carry out "not just our strategy [for the military campaign against the Islamic State] over the next two or three months, but our strategy going forward."[10] It could be argued, however, that even if limitations are enacted and perceived later to have a deleterious effect on the U.S. campaign against the Islamic State, such limitations could be removed or modified through subsequent legislative action if the need arises. Such limitations and an overall lack of flexibility in any IS AUMF, however, might be difficult to change legislatively if Members of Congress cannot agree to changes; neither the 2001 nor 2002 AUMF has been amended, for example, despite the stated need for amendments by observers and Members over the lifespan of those two measures.

The following sections address some specific aspects of an AUMF that may come under debate in the 114th Congress.

Authorization Purpose and Scope

Some observers and Members of Congress have argued that recent open-ended, broadly worded authorizations can empower a President to continue military operations outside of Congress's intent. An IS AUMF could include language in the authorizing provision identifying the specific purpose for and scope of the President's use of U.S. military force, narrowing or broadening the President's flexibility. An authorization that authorizes force to defend "U.S. national security" against the threat posed by the Islamic State would seem to provide a broad "national security" basis for possible long-term, open-ended military operations. Authorizing force to protect U.S. "interests" generally would seem to provide even wider authority to the President, while including the goal of protecting both the United States and U.S. allies could expand the range of purposes for military action. As to scope, many past AUMFs include language stating that the President can use all "necessary and appropriate" force to achieve the purpose of the authorization. While this could provide the President with the flexibility he needs to effectively employ U.S. Armed Forces, such language leaves the determination of the form and extent of U.S. military force generally to the President. Congress could decide to place limitations and conditions on any broader purpose and scope provisions in an attempt to shape the President's use of U.S. military force. (See "Limitations and Conditions," below.)

Identifying Targeted Entities

Any new IS AUMF would be expected to name the Islamic State (or one of its other monikers, including ISIS, ISIL, or Daesh) as the primary entity to be targeted by authorized U.S. military force. As evidenced by the implementation of the 2001 AUMF, however, a number of issues arise in determining exactly who can be lawfully targeted under such a provision, and the extent to which Congress desires to define and/or limit the universe of lawful targets in an IS AUMF. First, while specifically targeting the Islamic State provides a basic starting point for determining authorized targets, in many cases it might be unclear whether individuals are in fact part of the Islamic State, are part of groups fighting alongside the Islamic State, or are merely part of nonaligned groups also fighting in the region, either against the United States and its allies or otherwise. Congress might also wish to include language providing for future iterations of the structure of the Islamic State group. The Islamic State might splinter at multiple points in time into several new entities with different names and different affiliations, or combine with other groups to form new entities. Indeed, the Islamic State itself was formerly known, among other things, as Al Qaeda in Iraq (AQI), and its former close relationship and subsequent reported split with Al Qaeda has complicated determinations of whether the 2001 AUMF could be applied against it. An IS AUMF could include language that extends the authority to use military force against any successor entities of the Islamic State.

Perhaps the aspect of identifying lawful targeted entities considered most fraught is the matter of "associated forces." One of the central criticisms of the application of authority in the 2001 AUMF has been the expansion of military force to target entities that successive Administrations have designated "co-belligerent" with Al Qaeda and the Taliban. In the context of the current campaign against the Islamic State, the Obama Administration has asserted that the Islamic State can be targeted as it can be considered a branch or in some ways a successor to Al Qaeda.[11] It can be argued that this opens the possibility of military force being used now and in the future against a number of groups associated with the Islamic State, further expanding the universe of targeted entities, possibly in countries other than Iraq and Syria.

Some recent IS AUMF proposals have attempted to better define what constitutes "associated forces," or requires presidential reporting on or certification of newly designated associated forces, in an attempt to circumscribe the number of lawfully targeted entities and ensure congressional input into any expansion of such entities. The term "associated forces" would seem to apply to forces that are not part of IS forces but are fighting in concert with such forces. Some proposals, however, such as the President's IS AUMF proposal, include language that seems to define both IS and associated forces, stating the term means "individuals and organizations fighting for, on behalf of, or alongside ISIL.... " This language might be seen as overly broad and vague; Members of Congress may desire to more precisely define the term, ensuring that only those forces that are determined to directly engage in military operations in cooperation with IS forces are lawfully targeted under any IS AUMF. On the other hand, given the President's stated policies of defending U.S. national security, stabilizing and maintaining a democratic Iraq, and supporting moderate Syrian groups fighting the Syrian forces of the Asad government, an IS AUMF could eschew the "associated forces" term in favor of targeting the Islamic State and any other individuals or groups that pose a threat to those policies.

Limitations and Conditions

In considering any proposals to limit the authority of an IS AUMF, for example, by prohibiting the use of ground forces or constraining operations to a certain geographic area, Congress must weigh competing interests. The President's proposal would not allow "enduring offensive ground combat operations," while several previous IS AUMF proposals prohibited the use of ground combat forces or operations with specific carve-outs regarding special forces and training, among other units/operations. Understanding the expected effect of these different provisions would likely be key to Congress's decision on including them into a finalized IS AUMF. The limitation on the use of ground forces or prohibiting ground combat operations might, as some argue, significantly restrict the ability of the President and U.S. military leadership to prosecute conflict against the Islamic State in the manner they feel is most effective. Some in Congress might consider such restriction acceptable, however, if it is determined to avoid the involvement of the U.S. Armed Forces in another large-scale ground conflict following so closely upon the end of two such conflicts in Iraq and Afghanistan.

A geographic limitation might hinder the President's ability to strike IS and associated forces in countries other than Iraq and Syria, despite these forces' proven ability to cross state borders when it suits their purposes. In addition, as more groups pledge to fight alongside the Islamic State, or identify themselves as parts of the Islamic State itself, in countries such as Egypt, Libya, Algeria, Saudi Arabia, and Yemen, it could be reasonably expected that the President might determine that U.S. military operations should expand outside Iraq and Syria in the future. Congress, however, might wish to include such a limitation to prevent a similar geographic expansion of military operations to the President's expansion under the 2001 AUMF's authority to several countries other than Afghanistan.

Repealing Previous AUMFs and Sunset Provisions

The President's proposal includes a three-year sunset provision automatically terminating the IS-specific authorization; H.J.Res. 27 would terminate the new authorization and repeal the 2001 AUMF after three years. There is concern that Congress placing time limitations on the campaigns against the Islamic State, as well as Al Qaeda and other terrorist groups targeted under the 2001 AUMF, would send the wrong message to such targeted groups and the world about U.S. resolve to defeat these groups. On the other hand, a sunset on authority to use military force could be utilized to ensure that the IS and 2001 AUMF authorizations are not interpreted to authorize the use of military force in perpetuity, and in a manner that some perceive as outside the scope and intent of the original authorizations. Given the Obama Administration's continuing reliance on that authorization to conduct the current campaign against the Islamic State, for example, leaving the 2001 AUMF in place without amendment might be a continuing source of confusion and contention concerning presidential authority to use military force against the Islamic State, and in Iraq, Syria, and the Middle East/North Africa region in general. In any case, some argue, automatic terminations of authority might force Congress to reconsider previous AUMFs and their provisions in light of changed circumstances, amending and reauthorizing as Congress sees necessary.

Reporting and Certification

Although the President has provided information both publicly and in briefings to Members of Congress concerning the campaign against the Islamic State, Congress may decide to require the President to report to Congress both before a new authorization can enter into effect, and at regular intervals as the campaign moves forward. Ensuring Congress is being presented with substantive, up-to-date information might serve to mitigate concerns over unchecked expansion of the scope and duration of military operations taken under any IS AUMF. The President's proposal would require general reporting on the actions taken under the authorization every six months, which is in line with the existing reporting requirements in the War Powers Resolution.[12] Previous IS AUMF proposals have contained more frequent and detailed reporting requirements.[13] Members of Congress might wish to have clear strategy presented before agreeing to authorize military force, requiring a report explaining such a strategy to Congress (such as the report required in H.J.Res. 30), and make it a condition of authorization. Periodic reporting could require updated information on the effectiveness of previously stated strategy, and the extent to which strategic goals are being achieved.

APPENDIX. COMPARISON OF IS AUMF PROPOSALS FROM THE 113TH CONGRESS[14]

Near the end of the 113th Congress, a number of Members proposed several new authorizations to use military force against the Islamic State:

Table A-1. Proposed Authorizations to Use Force Against the Islamic State

Bill or Resolution	Title	Sponsor	Date Introduced
H.R. 5415	Authorization for Use of Military Force against International Terrorism Act	Representative Frank Wolf	September 8, 2014
H.J.Res. 123	Authorization for the Use of Military Force Against the Islamic State of Iraq and the Levant (ISIL)	Representative Darrell Issa	September 8, 2014
S.J.Res. 42	Authorization for Use of Military Force against the Islamic State in Iraq and the Levant	Senator Bill Nelson	September 8, 2014
S.J.Res. 43	Authorization for Use of Force Against the Organization Called the Islamic State	Senator James Inhofe	September 8, 2014
S.J.Res. 44	Authorization for Use of Military Force against the Islamic State in Iraq and the Levant	Senator Tim Kaine	September 8, 2014
H.J.Res. 125	Authorization for Use of Military Force Against ISIL Resolution	Representative Adam Schiff	September 16, 2014
H.J.Res. 128	Authorization for Use of Military Force Against ISIL Resolution	Representative John Larson	September 19, 2014
S.J.Res. 47	Authorization for the Use of Military Force against the Islamic State of Iraq and the Levant	Senator Robert Menendez	December 13, 2014

Note: Each proposal was referred to either the House Foreign Affairs Committee or Senate Foreign Relations Committee, except H.J.Res. 128, which was referred to both the House Foreign Affairs and House Rules Committees, and S.J.Res. 47, which originated in the Senate Foreign Relations Committee and was reported favorably to the full Senate.

The analysis provided below compares similar types of provisions included in IS AUMF proposals from the 113th Congress and issues related to those provisions. *Table A-2* provides a breakdown of seven out of eight of these proposals by type of provision. Treatment of S.J.Res. 47 is included in the section entitled "Calls for a New AUMF and Congressional Action in the 113th Congress" in the main text of this report.

Scope of Force and Military Activities Authorized

All but one of the proposed IS AUMFs listed above are substantially similar in their description of the scope of authorized force, stating that the President is authorized to use "necessary and appropriate force." Two of the proposals grant the President the authority to determine what type and degree of force is necessary and appropriate, while four others state that "necessary and appropriate force" is authorized, without stating who is authorized to make such a determination. H.J.Res. 125 does not limit the scope of the use of force in this way, however, stating that the President is authorized to "use the Armed Forces of the United States," without requiring such use of force to be "necessary and appropriate" as determined by the President or otherwise. While it might be expected that the President, as Commander in Chief, will make the "necessary and appropriate" determination in all cases regardless, explicitly granting the President that role in the authorization might preclude congressional challenges to presidential decision making after an authorization is enacted.

S.J.Res. 44 also specifies the scope of military activities authorized and the objective of those activities. Under this proposed IS AUMF, the President is authorized "to participate in a campaign of airstrikes ... to degrade and defeat ISIL.... " Coupled with a general prohibition against the President's use of ground troops against the Islamic State, this provision might be effective in preventing expansion of the military activities that the President might utilize against IS forces.

Targeted Entities

Each of the proposed IS AUMFs identifies the Islamic State (using that moniker or one of the ISIS/ISIL aliases) as the target of authorized U.S. military force. S.J.Res. 43 specifies "ISIL" but also "any successor organization" to the Islamic State. S.J.Res. 44 extends the authorization to IS-associated forces, subject to the President's identification of such groups to Congress through a certification process set out in the resolution. While these provisions seem straightforwardly effective in ensuring they authorize force against the Islamic State, they might be considered less than sufficient in their coverage of the overall situation in Iraq and Syria. In late September, President Obama notified Congress of strikes against IS forces in Syria, but also made a separate notification of airstrikes in that country against the "Khorasan Group," identified by the President as part of Al Qaeda. If Congress intends to enact an AUMF to direct the President to conduct military activities in Iraq and Syria, it might craft authorization language that can encompass non-IS associated groups, of which the Khorasan group might be an example. On the other hand, Congress might choose to deliberately exclude such groups from a new authorization.

H.R. 5415 includes the Islamic State as a target, but also covers a number of other named terrorist groups and expansive categories of terrorist threats. The lawful targets of the bill include

> those countries, organizations, or persons associated with or supporting terrorist groups, including al Qaeda and its regional affiliates, the Islamic State of Iraq and Syria, al Shabaab, Boko Haram, and any other emerging regional terrorist groups that share a common violent extremist ideology with such terrorist groups, regional affiliates, or emerging terrorist groups....

This broad language would significantly expand the authorized use of military force not only with regard to the current crisis with the Islamic State in Iraq and Syria, but also in terms of U.S. counterterrorism activities worldwide. The authorization seems to include every state, other entity, or person that is part of or supporting a terrorist group, authorizing use of U.S. Armed Forces against each. In this regard, H.R. 5415 would seem to essentially serve as an expansive replacement for the authorities in the 2001 AUMF, delinking U.S. military action from the September 11, 2001, attacks that serve as some limitation on the use of military force in that earlier authorization.

Purpose of Authorization

Most of the proposed IS AUMFs state that their purpose, at least in part, is to "defend the national security of the United States" against the Islamic State. Some of these proposals include additional elements, however, that expand the purpose past U.S. national security. S.J.Res. 44, for example, states that the authorization is also intended to protect the United States and "other countries" from terrorist attacks. Should the Islamic State expand its operations or shift its tactics toward an expansive transnational terrorist agenda, such authorization could prove to be far reaching. S.J.Res. 44 also authorizes the use of force to "protect individuals from acts of violence in clear contravention of international law and basic human rights...." Read as an additional purpose to authorize the use of military force against IS forces, this language might be read to allow the President to use U.S. Armed Forces to fight the Islamic State even in cases where the United States is not facing a threat to its security. If the additional language were interpreted to be a second purpose, the authorization could be read to include military action against actors other than the Islamic State in order to stop human rights violations, greatly increasing the scope of the authorization.

Another proposal, S.J.Res. 42, does not include the "defend the national security" language, instead stating the authorization's purpose is "to prevent terrorist attacks on the people and interests of the United States and our allies." While the focus on the prevention of terrorist attacks is arguably more limited than a general protection of undefined national security interests, the inclusion of protecting of U.S. "interests" and allies generally from such attacks could be seen as broadening the authorization beyond the "U.S. national security" language of other proposals. Limiting the purpose to preventing terrorist attacks also might narrow the authorization insofar as it would not necessarily include a broader purpose to "defeat" the Islamic State completely or stop the Islamic State's ability to operate in a non-ally state such as Syria. H.R. 5415 has similar purpose language to that of S.J.Res. 42, but also states it is also the authorization's purpose "to eliminate" a wide range of terrorist groups (explained in the "Targeted Entities" section, above). This purpose language, therefore, might not require a known threat to the United States or its allies prior to the President using military force against a terrorist group. Criteria for assessing the "defeat" or "elimination" of targeted entities are not included.

Conditions on Use of Military Force

Three of the proposals include authorization language that states the President has authority to use military force when the United States is part of an effort by the broader international community, or part thereof, to meet the threat posed by the Islamic State. H.R. 5415 states that the President may use military force "with the close consultation, coordination, and cooperation with NATO and regional allies.... " S.J.Res. 44 authorizes the President to use military force "as part of a multinational coalition.... " H.J.Res. 128 includes two authorizing provisions, one of which seems to be intended to operate when the U.N. Security Council has passed a resolution authorizing its membership to use force against the Islamic State. Although each of these proposals seems to indicate an intent to ensure the United States does not use military force without international support, it is difficult to say whether the language might strictly require such multilateral action, or to what extent cooperation and coordinated action with other nations might be required.

Limitations on Use of Military Force

The proposed IS AUMFs contain a number of provisions intended to limit the authority to use military force. Some of the proposals include language excluding the deployment of U.S. ground troops from the President's authority, except for certain types of military units or to carry out certain activities. These proposals include language excluding authority for "deployment of ground forces in a combat role," "Armed Forces in direct combat operations," "rotational ground forces," or "United States ground combat forces." Each of these descriptions might be interpreted to affect the President's authority differently. Excluding deployment of ground forces "in a combat role" might be more restrictive than excluding forces that engage in "direct combat operations," as there might be combat roles for U.S. Armed Forces that do not fall within the interpretation of the term "direct." A number of types of ground combat forces might also fall outside the definition of "rotational" ground forces. These differences in language might result in authorizations with limitations on presidential authority of varied effectiveness. In addition, two of the proposed IS AUMFs provide exceptions to the limitation on ground troops. H.J.Res. 125 would allow deployment of ground troops that are "special operations forces" or forces "deployed in a training, advisory, or intelligence capacity." While these exceptions might still exclude most U.S. Armed Forces units from deployment under the proposed AUMF, the overall number of troops that could be deployed under the exceptions could be sizeable, and their roles could place them in harm's way in many cases. S.J.Res. 44 also includes exceptions to the ban on ground troops, allowing deployments for military assistance and training, protection or rescue of U.S. Armed Forces or citizens, and "limited operations against high value targets."

H.J.Res. 125 and S.J.Res. 44 also include geographic limitations to their respective overall authority to use military force. Both limit that authority to Iraq and Syria.[15] In light of the Islamic State's expansive ambitions and operations close to the borders of Turkey, Jordan, Lebanon, and potentially other countries, such language could prove more restrictive in an evolving conflict than might be initially assumed. In the context of implementation of recent AUMFs, especially the 2001 AUMF, such limitations seem to be important, as successive Presidents have interpreted the 2001 AUMF to allow for use of military force in multiple countries that might not have been contemplated when Congress enacted the original authorization. S.J.Res. 44 also limits any use of force against IS associated forces, stating that there is no authority to use force against those forces unless the President identifies such forces in periodic reports to Congress. Again, this seems to be a response to the executive branch's implementation of the 2001 AUMF; both President Bush and Obama have independently interpreted that authority to extend to associated forces that are "co-belligerents" with Al Qaeda and the Taliban, including forces in multiple countries outside the original target of U.S. military action, Afghanistan.

Five of the proposed IS AUMFs include a provision that automatically terminates their respective authorizations after a certain period of time, with sunset provisions of 120 days, one year, 18 months, two years, and three years.

S.J.Res. 44 also includes an interpretive provision, stating that its authorization should not be construed as "authorizing support for force in support of, or in cooperation with, the national government of Syria ... or its security services.... "

Repeal of Previous AUMFs

Four of the proposals would repeal the 2002 AUMF authorizing the use of military force against Iraq. Two of these four, H.J.Res. 125 and H.J.Res. 128, would also repeal the 2001 AUMF with a delay, with repeal taking effect 18 months and two years after enactment, respectively. The Obama Administration had recently adopted the position both that the 2002 AUMF could be repealed without detriment to U.S. Armed Forces or U.S. interests, and that the 2001 AUMF could be amended or repealed once the planned U.S. Armed Forces withdrawal from Afghanistan was completed and a bilateral security agreement with Afghanistan is finalized.[16] These repeal provisions seem to generally correspond with these recent Administration positions. Recent statements by the Obama Administration and the President's September 23, 2014, notification to Congress of strikes against IS forces, however, indicate that the President considers the 2001 and 2002 AUMFs as authority to conduct a military campaign against the Islamic State as well as other Al Qaeda-related groups. Given this presidential application of existing AUMFs, the repeal provisions might take on the role of repudiating the President's positions on his existing authority to use military force against the Islamic State and other terrorist groups. Repeal of these AUMFs could be seen as an indication that Congress disagrees with the President's interpretation of his existing authorities to use force and that it intends to replace his existing authority with a possibly narrower authority in an IS AUMF.

Reporting and Certification Requirements

Five of the proposed IS AUMFs require presidential reporting to Congress to include various information, including

- the Administration's strategy for military action against the Islamic State and in Iraq and Syria generally, and implementation of or changes to the strategy;
- the status of military actions taken under a given authorization;
- descriptions of plans for further military action, as well as redeployment of U.S. Armed Forces after military action is completed;
- expenditures made pursuant to the authorization, or the budgetary effects of military action taken; and
- the status and actions of any multinational coalition cooperating with the United States to engage the Islamic State and other groups militarily.

S.J.Res. 44 requires the President to report to Congress every 90 days on his identification of IS associated forces in order to gain the authority to use military force against such associated forces. In order for the President to have authority to use military force without a relevant U.N. Security Council resolution, H.J.Res. 128 requires the President to certify that the United States sought approval of such a resolution, that the Security Council is unlikely to approve such a resolution, and that the President has instead sought to build a broad coalition of nations to counter the IS threat.

War Powers Resolution and Expedited Consideration Provisions

Each of the proposals states that its respective provision authorizing the use of military force is intended to constitute specific statutory authorization within the meaning of Section 5(b) of the War Powers Resolution (WPR; P.L. 93-148; 50 U.S.C. §§1541-1548). Section 5(b) of the WPR states that the President shall withdraw U.S. Armed Forces from active or imminent hostilities within 60 days after a presidential notification of the introduction of U.S. Armed Forces into such hostilities is made or is required to be made under Section 4(a)(1) of the WPR, unless Congress has enacted a declaration of war or authorization to use military force, among other exceptions. The statement that these proposals are intended to act as authorization under the WPR might indicate Congress's desire to approve the President's current military actions, within the scope and limitations explained above. Although the President ordered the first airstrikes against IS forces in early August, there does not seem to be clear consensus among experts or Members of Congress on when the 60-day period began running, and whether it is running currently. The President's reliance on the existing AUMFs to conduct military operations against the Islamic State and other groups in Iraq and Syria, if accepted by Congress, would have stopped any running of the 60-day clock, whether or not a new IS AUMF is enacted, as there would be existing congressional authorization for his actions.

Section 6 of the WPR provides for expedited consideration of legislative proposals introduced in accordance with Section 5(b); it is not apparent that any of the current IS AUMF proposals are currently being subjected to these expedited procedures. Although the WPR sets out these procedures in legislation, such procedural provisions do not take precedence over the rulemaking and procedural prerogatives of either house of Congress, and each house maintains the authority to enforce its own rules at its discretion.[17] H.J.Res. 128 sets out its own procedures for expedited consideration of a further resolution authorizing military force against the Islamic State, if such resolution meets H.J.Res. 128's definition of a "qualified resolution." The process is described in *Table A-2* below, in the "Expedited Consideration" section.

Table A-2. Proposed Authorizations for Use of Military Force Against the Islamic State in the 113th Congress Comparison of Similar Provisions (as of October 20, 2014)

Provision	H.R. 5415	H.J.Res. 123	H.J.Res. 125	H.J.Res. 128[a] *with U.N. Security Council Resolution*	H.J.Res. 128[a] *without U.N. Security Council Resolution*	S.J.Res. 42	S.J.Res. 43	S.J.Res. 44
Scope of authorized force	"The President is authorized ... to use all necessary and appropriate force"	"The President is authorized to use the Armed Forces of the United States as the President determines to be necessary and appropriate"	"The President is authorized to use the Armed Forces of the United States"	"The President is authorized to use the United States Armed Forces as the President determines to be necessary and appropriate"	Same, except subject to conditions (see Reporting/Certification row, below) and enactment of a second joint resolution under expedited procedures	"The President is authorized to use appropriate force"	"the President is authorized to use all necessary and appropriate force"	"the President is authorized ... to use all necessary and appropriate force"
International conditions for use of force	"with the close consultation, coordination,	none specified	none specified	U.N. Security Council resolution	No U.N. Security Council resolution authorizing use of force against ISIL	none specified	none specified	"as part of a multinational coalition"

Table A-2. (Continued)

Provision	H.R. 5415	H.J.Res. 123	H.J.Res. 125	H.J.Res. 128[a] *with U.N. Security Council Resolution*	H.J.Res. 128[a] *without U.N. Security Council Resolution*	S.J.Res. 42	S.J.Res. 43	S.J.Res. 44
	and cooperation with NATO and regional allies”			authorizing use of force against ISIL				
Types of military action authorized	none specified	none specified	none specified	none specified	none specified	none specified	none specified	“to participate in a campaign of airstrikes in Iraq, and if the President deems necessary, in Syria, to degrade and defeat ISIL” The resolution would also authorize the President to “provide military equipment and

Provision	H.R. 5415	H.J.Res. 123	H.J.Res. 125	H.J.Res. 128[a] *with U.N. Security Council Resolution*	H.J.Res. 128[a] *without U.N. Security Council Resolution*	S.J.Res. 42	S.J.Res. 43	S.J.Res. 44
								training to forces fighting ISIL in Iraq or Syria"
Target of use of military force	"those countries, organizations, or persons associated with or supporting terrorist groups, including al Qaeda and its regional affiliates, the Islamic State of Iraq and Syria, al Shabaab, Boko Haram, and any other emerging	"Islamic State of Iraq and the Levant (ISIL)"	"Islamic State of Iraq and the Levant (ISIL)"	"Islamic State of Iraq and the Levant ('ISIL')"	"Islamic State of Iraq and the Levant ('ISIL')"	"Islamic State of Iraq and the Levant (ISIL)"	"Islamic State (or "IS"), formally known as the Islamic State of Iraq and the Levant, as well as any successor organization"	"Islamic State in Iraq and the Levant (ISIL)", as well as ISIL-associated forces, subject to requirements in Section 4 (see below)

Table A-2. (Continued)

Provision	H.R. 5415	H.J.Res. 123	H.J.Res. 125	H.J.Res. 128[a] *with U.N. Security Council Resolution*	H.J.Res. 128[a] *without U.N. Security Council Resolution*	S.J.Res. 42	S.J.Res. 43	S.J.Res. 44
	regional terrorist groups that share a common violent extremist ideology with such terrorist groups, regional affiliates, or emerging terrorist groups"							
Purpose	"to eliminate all such terrorist groups and prevent any future	"to defend the national security of the United States against the	none specified	"to ... defend the national security of the United States	"to defend the national security of the United States against the Islamic State of Iraq and the Levant ('ISIL')"	"to prevent terrorist attacks on the people and interests of the United States and our	"to defend the national security of the United States against the threat posed by	"to protect the United States and other countries from terrorist attacks by the

Provision	H.R. 5415	H.J.Res. 123	H.J.Res. 125	H.J.Res. 128[a] *with U.N. Security Council Resolution*	H.J.Res. 128[a] *without U.N. Security Council Resolution*	S.J.Res. 42	S.J.Res. 43	S.J.Res. 44
	acts of international terrorism against the United States or its allies by such terrorist groups, countries, organization, or persons”	continuing threat posed by the Islamic State of Iraq and the Levant (ISIL)”		against the Islamic State of Iraq and the Levant (‘ISIL’); and enforce a United Nations Security Council resolution” that authorizes a multilateral coalition to take several types of action against ISIL		allies”	the organization called the Islamic State (or ‘IS’), formally known as the Islamic State of Iraq and the Levant, as well as any successor organization”	Islamic State in Iraq and the Levant (ISIL), and in order to protect individuals from acts of violence in clear contravention of international law and basic human rights”

Table A-2. (Continued)

Provision	H.R. 5415	H.J.Res. 123	H.J.Res. 125	H.J.Res. 128[a] *with U.N. Security Council Resolution*	H.J.Res. 128[a] *without U.N. Security Council Resolution*	S.J.Res. 42	S.J.Res. 43	S.J.Res. 44
Geographic limitation	none specified	none specified	"authority ... shall be confined to the territory of the Republic of Iraq and the Syrian Arab Republic" Limitation does not apply to foreign military training activities	none specified		none specified	none specified	Authorization applies to Iraq and Syria
Military unit	none	none	"does not	none	use of U.S. Armed	"does not	none specified	"does not

Provision	H.R. 5415	H.J.Res. 123	H.J.Res. 125	H.J.Res. 128[a] *with U.N. Security Council Resolution*	H.J.Res. 128[a] *without U.N. Security Council Resolution*	S.J.Res. 42	S.J.Res. 43	S.J.Res. 44
limitation	specified	specified	include the authority for the deployment of ground forces in a combat role" Limitation does not apply to "special operations forces or other forces that may be deployed in a training, advisory, or intelligence capacity"	specified	Forces authorized "other than the use of such Armed Forces in direct ground combat operations"	include authorization for the use of rotational ground forces"		include ... use of United States ground combat forces, except for [military assistance and training] or as necessary for the protection or rescue of members of the United States Armed Forces or United States citizens..., or for limited operations against high value targets"

Table A-2. (Continued)

Provision	H.R. 5415	H.J.Res. 123	H.J.Res. 125	H.J.Res. 128[a] *with U.N. Security Council Resolution*	H.J.Res. 128[a] *without U.N. Security Council Resolution*	S.J.Res. 42	S.J.Res. 43	S.J.Res. 44
Targeting associated forces limitation	none specified	none specified	none specified	none specified	none specified	none specified	none specified	"does not include ... authorization for the use of force against forces associated with ISIL, unless such forces are identified in a report submitted under section 4" of the resolution.
Government of Syria limitation	none	none	none	none	none	none	none	"Nothing in this resolution shall be

Provision	H.R. 5415	H.J.Res. 123	H.J.Res. 125	H.J.Res. 128[a] *with U.N. Security Council Resolution*	H.J.Res. 128[a] *without U.N. Security Council Resolution*	S.J.Res. 42	S.J.Res. 43	S.J.Res. 44
								construed as ... authorizing support for force in support of, or in cooperation with, the national government of Syria ... or its security services"
Sunset	none	120 days after date of enactment	18 months after date of enactment	2 years		3 years after date of enactment	none	1 year from date of enactment
AUMF Repeal	none	Resolution would repeal 2002 AUMF	Resolution would repeal 2002 AUMF immediately, and repeal	Resolution would repeal 2002 AUMF immediately, and repeal the 2001 AUMF 2 years after date of enactment		none	none	Resolution would repeal 2002 AUMF

Table A-2. (Continued)

Provision	H.R. 5415	H.J.Res. 123	H.J.Res. 125	H.J.Res. 128[a] *with U.N. Security Council Resolution*	H.J.Res. 128[a] *without U.N. Security Council Resolution*	S.J.Res. 42	S.J.Res. 43	S.J.Res. 44
			the 2001 AUMF 18 months after date of enactment					
Reporting/ Certification	none	Not later than 60 days after enactment, President is required to report on "status of all actions taken"; "description of all proposed actions"; "status of	"The President shall, at least once every 60 days" after enactment, report on relevant matters including actions taken and planned	none specified	President must certify that the United States has sought, but the United Nations Security Council has not approved, a resolution authorizing the use of force, and is unlikely to; and that the President has sought to build a broad international coalition to counter ISIL President must	none	Not later than 15 days after enactment, President is required to submit comprehensive strategy to defeat the Islamic State; not later than 90 days after the first report is required,	Section 4 requires the President to identify ISILassociated forces targetable under the resolution in a report every 90 days

Provision	H.R. 5415	H.J.Res. 123	H.J.Res. 125	H.J.Res. 128[a] *with U.N. Security Council Resolution*	H.J.Res. 128[a] *without U.N. Security Council Resolution*	S.J.Res. 42	S.J.Res. 43	S.J.Res. 44
		engagement of allies of the United States and international coalitions in combating" ISIL; and "estimated budgetary effects of actions proposed"	actions under the authorization		present a strategy for use of military force against ISIL		President must report on implementation of the strategy; any substantive change to strategy requires an immediate additional report	
				In both cases, every 60 days the President must report on uses of lethal force and their circumstances, civilian casualties resulting from such use of force, estimate of expenditures resulting from the use of force, and planning for redeployment of U.S. Armed Forces after military action against ISIL is				

Table A-2. (Continued)

Provision	H.R. 5415	H.J.Res. 123	H.J.Res. 125	H.J.Res. 128[a] *with U.N. Security Council Resolution*	H.J.Res. 128[a] *without U.N. Security Council Resolution*	S.J.Res. 42	S.J.Res. 43	S.J.Res. 44
				Completed				
Consultation	none specified	none specified	none specified	"The President shall consult on a regular basis with the congressional committees of jurisdiction to provide updated information on actions being taken pursuant to this joint resolution in either public or closed sessions"		none specified	none specified	none specified
War Powers Resolution	Bill states authorization section is "intended to constitute specific statutory authorization within the meaning of section 5(b) of	Resolution states authorization section is "intended to constitute specific statutory authorization within the meaning of	Resolution states authorization section is "intended to constitute specific statutory authorization within the meaning of section 5(b)	(in both cases) Resolution states that authorization sections are "intended to constitute specific authorization within the meaning of section 5(b) of the War Powers Resolution"		Resolution states authorization section is "intended to constitute specific statutory authorization within the meaning of section 5(b) of	Resolution states authorization section is "intended to constitute specific statutory authorization within the meaning of section 5(b) of	Resolution states authorization section is "intended to constitute specific statutory authorization within the meaning of section 5(b) of

Provision	H.R. 5415	H.J.Res. 123	H.J.Res. 125	H.J.Res. 128[a] *with U.N. Security Council Resolution*	H.J.Res. 128[a] *without U.N. Security Council Resolution*	S.J.Res. 42	S.J.Res. 43	S.J.Res. 44
	the War Powers Resolution"	section 5(b) of the War Powers Resolution"	of the War Powers Resolution"			the War Powers Resolution"	the War Powers Resolution"	the War Powers Resolution"
Expedited Consideration	none	none	none	none	Provides expedited consideration for a second resolution, if such resolution is introduced by the majority or minority leader in the House or Senate within the next legislative day after a required presidential certification is submitted. In both houses, second resolution is to be placed on the calendar, considered within one legislative day, debated for a maximum of 20 hours,	none	none	none

Table A-2. (Continued)

Provision	H.R. 5415	H.J.Res. 123	H.J.Res. 125	H.J.Res. 128[a] *with U.N. Security Council Resolution*	H.J.Res. 128[a] *without U.N. Security Council Resolution*	S.J.Res. 42	S.J.Res. 43	S.J.Res. 44
					and voted upon immediately following debate; passage of resolution in one chamber requires immediate action by the second chamber on the resolution received			

Source: Congress.gov.

[a] H.J.Res. 128 contains two separate authorization provisions. Section 3 of the resolution operates when the U.N. Security Council has adopted a resolution authorizing the use of military force against the Islamic State; Section 4 operates when no such resolution has been adopted. Section 4 does not in fact authorize the use of military force, but instead creates a process of presidential reporting and certification and expedited consideration procedures for a separate resolution to be introduced after such reporting and certification has been made to Congress. The table therefore sets out the operative provisions and language in H.J.Res. 128 in two columns to separate the operative language of the two authorization sections. For provisions that apply no matter which authorization section is operative, or where the resolution does not contain the type of provision being explained, the two columns are combined.

End Notes

[1] For more information and analysis of the IS crisis, the U.S. response, and related issues, see CRS Report R43612, The "Islamic State" Crisis and U.S. Policy, by Kenneth Katzman et al.; and CRS Report R43720, U.S. Military Action Against the Islamic State: Answers to Frequently Asked Legal Questions, by Michael John Garcia and Jennifer K. Elsea.

[2] Available at http://www.whitehouse.gov/the-press-office/2014/09/23/letter-president-war-powers-resolutionregarding-iraq; http://www.whitehouse.gov/the-press-office/2014/09/23/letter-president-war-powers-resolutionregarding-syria.

[3] President Barack Obama, remarks at a press conference, November 5, 2014, http://www.whitehouse.gov/the-pressoffice/2014/11/05/remarks-president-press-conference.

[4] Testimony of Stephen W. Preston, General Counsel, Department of Defense, before the Senate Committee on Foreign Relations, hearing on the Authorization for Use of Military Force, 113th Cong., 2nd sess., May 21, 2014, http://www.foreign.senate.gov/imo /media/doc/Preston_Testimony.pdf.

[5] White House, "Press Briefing by Press Secretary Josh Earnest," press release, September 11, 2014, http://www.whitehouse.gov/the-press-office/2014/09/11/press-briefing-press-secretary-josh-earnest-9112014.

[6] Testimony of Secretary of State John Kerry, U.S. Congress, Senate Committee on Foreign Relations, Authorization For The Use of Military Force Against ISIL, 113th Cong., 2nd sess., December 11, 2014.

[7] This definition is the exact language included in the President's IS AUMF proposal. See "The President's February 2015 IS AUMF Proposal," below.

[8] Available at http://www.cq.com/doc/4622425?0&pos=alert&dlvid=115410051&agenttype=13.

[9] President Barack Obama, Letter from the President—Authorization for the Use of United States Armed Forces in connection with the Islamic State of Iraq and the Levant, February 11, 2015, http://www.whitehouse.gov/the-pressoffice/2015/02/11/letter-president-authorization-use-united-states-armed-forces-connection.

[10] President Barack Obama, remarks at a press conference, November 5, 2014, http://www.whitehouse.gov/the-pressoffice/2014/11/05/remarks-president-press-conference.

[11] See "Press Briefing by Press Secretary Josh Earnest," supra note 5.

[12] See Section 4(c) of the War Powers Resolution (P.L. 93-148; 50 U.S.C. § 1543(c)).

[13] See Table A-2 in the Appendix, below.

[14] This section does not include proposals introduced earlier in the 113th Congress that would, for example, repeal existing AUMFs or express a sense-of-Congress about military action in Iraq and/or Syria. Another proposal, H.J.Res. 127, introduced September 8, 2014, would recognize a state of war exists between the United States and the Islamic State, and authorize the use of military force against the Islamic State and associated forces.

[15] H.J.Res. 125 states that the limitation does not apply to foreign military training, although this type of activity would not be expected to raise questions concerning the authority to use military force.

[16] See testimony of Mary McLeod and Stephen Preston, U.S. Congress, Senate Committee on Foreign Relations, hearing on Authorization for Use of Military Force, 113th Cong., 2nd sess., May 21, 2014.

[17] For more information, see CRS Report 98-888, "Fast-Track" or Expedited Procedures: Their Purposes, Elements, and Implications, by Christopher M. Davis; CRS Report RS20234, Expedited or "Fast-Track" Legislative Procedures, by Christopher M. Davis; CRS Report RL30599, Expedited Procedures in the House: Variations Enacted Into Law, by Christopher M. Davis.

In: Authorization for Use of Military Force ... ISBN: : 978-1-63483-556-5
Editor: Tomas Mendoza

Chapter 2

2001 AUTHORIZATION FOR USE OF MILITARY FORCE: ISSUES CONCERNING ITS CONTINUED APPLICATION*

Matthew C. Weed

SUMMARY

In response to the September 11, 2001, terrorist attacks against the United States, Congress enacted the Authorization for Use of Military Force (2001 AUMF; P.L. 107-40; 50 U.S.C. §1541 note) to authorize the use of military force against those who perpetrated or provided support for the attacks. Under the authority of the 2001 AUMF, U.S. Armed Forces have conducted military operations in Afghanistan since October 2001. As armed conflict against Al Qaeda and the Taliban progressed, and U.S. counterterrorism strategy evolved, U.S. use of military force has expanded outside Afghanistan to include Al Qaeda and Taliban targets in Pakistan, Yemen, Somalia, Libya, and most recently, Syria.

The 2001 AUMF is not the sole authority for all U.S. uses of military force in furtherance of U.S. counterterrorism objectives; other legislation and presidential powers under Article II of the Constitution are invoked to carry out U.S. counterterrorism activities globally. Nevertheless, the Obama Administration still finds itself relying on 2001 AUMF authority

* This is an edited, reformatted and augmented version of a Congressional Research Service publication R43983, prepared for Members and Committees of Congress, dated April 14, 2015.

not only for continuing U.S. military operations in Afghanistan, but also for beginning a new campaign against the Islamic State in Iraq and Syria, with the possibility of expansion to other countries if the Islamic State or Al Qaeda groups or associates effectively expand their reach and pose a threat to U.S. national security and interests. At the same time, the President has requested that Congress enact new authority for U.S. operations to counter the Islamic State and has expressed a continued commitment to "working with the Congress and the American people to refine, and ultimately repeal, the 2001 AUMF."

As the United States has engaged in counterterrorism and other military operations against Al Qaeda, the Taliban, and other terrorist and extremist groups over the past 13-plus years, many Members of Congress and legal and policy analysts have questioned the continuing reliance on the 2001 AUMF as a primary, effective authority for U.S. military action in a number of countries. Some have asserted that the 2001 AUMF has become outdated, unsuited to the challenge of countering terrorism and extremism in a changed world, at times claiming that the executive branch has relied on the 2001 AUMF for military action outside its intended scope.

Congress has for several years considered a number of legislative proposals to change the authority in the 2001 AUMF (by amending or repealing the law), the manner in which it is used, and the congressional role in its oversight and continuing existence. This process continues in the 114th Congress, and deliberations over the future of the 2001 AUMF have become entwined with consideration of proposals to enact a new authorization for use of military force to respond to the turmoil caused by the actions of the Islamic State in Iraq and Syria. Debate in Congress over the status of the 2001 AUMF may evolve in response to numerous developments overseas and U.S. policy responses.

INTRODUCTION

In response to the September 11, 2001, terrorist attacks against the United States, Congress enacted the Authorization for Use of Military Force (2001 AUMF; P.L. 107-40; 50 U.S.C. §1541 note) to authorize the use of military force against those who perpetrated or provided support for the attacks. President George W. Bush identified Al Qaeda as the group that carried out the attacks, and the Taliban, then in control of the governance of Afghanistan, as harboring Al Qaeda within the territory of that country. Under the authority of the 2001 AUMF, in October 2001 President Bush sent U.S. Armed Forces to Afghanistan to conduct military operations "designed to disrupt the use of Afghanistan as a terrorist base of operations and to attack the military capability of the Taliban regime."[1] More than 13 years later, in December 2014, President Obama declared the end of the combat mission in Afghanistan. Despite this announcement, U.S. Armed Forces remain in Afghanistan and are reportedly authorized to target Al Qaeda and the Taliban.[2]

As armed conflict against Al Qaeda and the Taliban has progressed, and U.S. counterterrorism strategy has evolved, U.S. use of military force has expanded outside Afghanistan. After the U.S. invasion of Afghanistan, many members of Al Qaeda moved out of the country and into Pakistan. In response, the United States has conducted unmanned aerial vehicle (UAV) missile strikes against Al Qaeda and Taliban targets in Pakistan. The United States has identified other groups in the Middle East and Africa that it considers "associated forces" of Al Qaeda, that is, organized forces that have entered alongside Al Qaeda in its armed conflict with the United States and its coalition partners. The United States has used force against these Al Qaeda associates in a number of other countries, including Yemen, Somalia, Libya, and most recently, Syria. In addition, the President has relied in part on the 2001 AUMF as authority for his campaign against the Islamic State (also known as ISIS or ISIL) in Iraq and Syria, and against the Khorosan Group of Al Qaeda in Syria. Since 2001, counterterrorism activities involving deployment of U.S. Armed Forces, if not always the use of military force, have steadily increased, taking place in countries around the world, although it is not clear whether the 2001 AUMF has provided authority for these activities.

The 2001 AUMF, as many have argued and the executive branch has agreed, does not seem to authorize all uses of military force in furtherance of U.S. counterterrorism objectives. Although some presidential reporting to Congress suggests a wide interpretation of the scope of 2001 AUMF authority, the Obama Administration, as recently as May 2014, has stated that the 2001 AUMF authorizes only those uses of military force against Al Qaeda, the Taliban, and their associated forces, and, when such actions are taken outside of Afghanistan, only in cases of imminent threat of attack against the United States.[3] Because the 2001 AUMF covers only some uses of military force to counter terrorist threats, other legislation and presidential powers under Article II of the Constitution provide authority to carry out U.S. counterterrorism activities globally. Some observers and Members of Congress have argued that the 2001 AUMF, focused as it is on those who perpetrated and supported the September 11, 2001, terrorist attacks, is outdated and should be repealed, as it has been stretched and perhaps distorted to fit uses of force that were not contemplated when the 2001 AUMF was enacted. Others assert that the 2001

AUMF should be updated to reflect the evolution of the terrorist threat since 2001 and the continued need to authorize the use of military force against this threat, perhaps with greater oversight and procedural requirements from Congress.

The Obama Administration has indicated its willingness to address concerns about the 2001 AUMF and continued uses of military force in support of counterterrorism goals, in the past arguing that the 2001 AUMF must remain in force until combat operations end in Afghanistan. By the end of 2014, the United States and Afghanistan had finalized a bilateral security agreement, and the combat mission in Afghanistan had been declared complete. The Obama Administration, however, still finds itself relying on 2001 AUMF authority not only for continuing U.S. military operations in Afghanistan, but also for beginning a new campaign against the Islamic State in Iraq and Syria, and possibly expanding operations to other countries if the Islamic State or Al Qaeda groups or associates effectively expand their reach and pose a threat to U.S. national security and interests. The President, in his February 11, 2015, letter to Congress concerning his draft proposal for a new authorization for use of military force against the Islamic State, stated, "I remain committed to working with the Congress and the American people to refine, and ultimately repeal, the 2001 AUMF."[4]

In the face of these issues, Congress has for several years considered a number of legislative proposals to change the authority in the 2001 AUMF, the manner in which it is used, and the congressional role in its oversight and continuing existence. This process has continued in the 114th Congress, and deliberations over the future of the 2001 AUMF have become entwined with consideration of proposals to enact a new AUMF to respond to the actions of the Islamic State in Iraq and Syria.

2001 AUMF Enactment, Interpretation, and Use

Generally considered a broad authorization for the President to use military force against the terrorist threat posed by Al Qaeda after the September 11, 2001, terrorist attacks, the 2001 AUMF is nonetheless limited in scope, targeting only those who perpetrated or supported those attacks. Because of this limitation, the two most recent Administrations have instituted procedures to determine which actors are lawful targets of military force and in which parts of the world such force might be used under different circumstances. The effect has been U.S. uses of military force or other deployment activities in several countries, and varying as to type and scope.

Legislative Background

Shortly after the September 11, 2001, terrorist attacks on the United States, Congress enacted and President George W. Bush signed into law the 2001 AUMF. The 2001 AUMF authorizes the President to use U.S. Armed Forces to combat the nations, groups, and individuals who perpetrated the September 11, 2001, attacks and those who harbored such perpetrators. Section 2(a) of the 2001 AUMF authorizes the use of force in response to the September 11 attacks:

> Resolved by the Senate and House of Representatives of the United States of America in Congress assembled,
>
> . . . .
>
> SEC. 2. AUTHORIZATION FOR USE OF UNITED STATES ARMED FORCES.
>
> (a) IN GENERAL.—That the President is authorized to use all necessary and appropriate force against those nations, organizations, or persons he determines planned, authorized, committed, or aided the terrorist attacks that occurred on September 11, 2001, or harbored such organizations or persons, in order to prevent any future acts of international terrorism against the United States by such nations, organizations or persons.

The authorizing language is broad in its scope concerning prevention of any future acts of terrorism perpetrated against the United States, but is circumscribed by authorizing the targeting only of those nations, organizations, or persons involved in perpetrating the September 11 attacks or harboring those who perpetrated the attacks. Although President Bush identified the terrorist group Al Qaeda and individuals within that group as the perpetrators of the attacks, and the Taliban then governing Afghanistan as the entity that harbored Al Qaeda, these actors were not specifically named in the 2001 AUMF's language. The 2001 AUMF represented a novel approach to modern-era military force authorizations, because it empowered the President to target non-state actors, even to the individual level, instead of only states.

In contrast to the authorization enacted by Congress in the 2001 AUMF, the legislation originally proposed by the Bush Administration in the wake of the September 11, 2001, attacks would have provided the authority to use military force not only against Al Qaeda and the Taliban, but also to counter all terrorist threats generally, without necessitating a connection to the attacks:

> Resolved by the Senate and the House of Representatives of the United States of America in Congress assembled—
>
> That the President is authorized to use all necessary and appropriate force against those nations, organizations or persons he determines planned, authorized, harbored, committed, or aided in the planning or commission of the attacks against the United States that occurred on September 11, 2001, and to deter and pre-empt any future acts of terrorism or aggression against the United States.[5]

Because Congress did not accept this broader authorization language, it can be argued that Congress deliberately chose to limit presidential authority to respond to the threat posed by those who carried out and supported the September 11, 2001, attacks, and not to other persons, nations, or groups. The continuing application of 2001 AUMF authority and its perceived expansion has led to arguments over the proper scope of 2001 AUMF authority and calls for legislative clarification of such scope.[6]

Interpretation

Because Congress limited the use of force to targets associated with the September 11, 2001, attacks, while according broad discretion to the President regarding whom to target, implementing the 2001 AUMF has required the creation of frameworks and procedures to determine which uses of force fall under the 2001 AUMF's authority.

Interpretation Prior to Summer 2014 Islamic State Crisis

Prior to the U.S. military campaign against the Islamic State that began in summer 2014, executive branch officials made statements that included certain interpretations[7] concerning the 2001 AUMF:

- The 2001 AUMF is primarily an authorization to enter into and prosecute an armed conflict against Al Qaeda and the Taliban in Afghanistan.
- The 2001 AUMF authorizes the President to use military force against Al Qaeda and the Taliban outside Afghanistan, but such uses of force must meet a higher standard of threat to the United States and must use limited, precise methods against specific individual targets rather than general military action against enemy forces.
- Because the 2001 AUMF authorizes U.S. involvement in an international armed conflict, the international law of armed conflict informs the authority within the 2001 AUMF. This law permits the use of military force against forces associated with Al Qaeda and the Taliban as co-belligerents; such forces must be operating in some sort of coordination and cooperation with Al Qaeda and/or the Taliban, not just share similar goals, objectives, or ideologies.

According to the Obama Administration, this interpretation of the scope of 2001 AUMF authority fits within the overall framework of presidential power to use military force against those posing a threat to U.S. national security and U.S. interests. In situations where the 2001 AUMF or other relevant legislation does not seem to authorize a given use of military force or related activity, the executive branch will determine whether the President's Article II powers as Commander in Chief and Chief Executive, as interpreted by the executive branch itself, might authorize such actions. In this way, similar U.S. military action to meet U.S. counterterrorism objectives might be interpreted to fall under different authorities, of which the 2001 AUMF is just one, albeit important, example.

Interpretation Applied to Military Campaign Against the Islamic State

In seeming contrast to the interpretation described above, Obama Administration officials and the President's September 2014 notifications[8] to Congress for airstrikes and other actions in Iraq and Syria stated that the 2001 AUMF authorizes the President to order certain U.S. military strikes against the Islamic State in Iraq and Syria,[9] as well as the Khorasan Group of Al Qaeda in Syria. This reliance on 2001 AUMF authority might represent a shift in the Administration's previously stated interpretation of that authority in at least two ways. First, the military campaign against the Islamic State seems to represent an expansion of the scope of military operations undertaken previously outside Afghanistan under 2001 AUMF authority. Second, the reasons for the military campaign seem to rest as much on (1) current U.S. policy goals for Iraq's stability; (2) the stability of the region; and (3) support for moderate rebel groups in their fight against the Islamic State, other extremist groups, and the Asad government in Syria, as they do on responding to an imminent threat to the United States, its citizens, or its personnel and facilities abroad.

Authorization for Use of Military Force Against Iraq Resolution of 2002

Separate from the 2001 AUMF enacted after the September 11, 2001, terrorist attacks, Congress enacted the Authorization for Use of Military Force Against Iraq Resolution of 2002 (2002 AUMF; P.L. 107-243) prior to the 2003 U.S. invasion of Iraq that toppled the government of Saddam Hussein, with U.S. military deployments to and operations in Iraq continuing until December 2011. The 2002 AUMF authorizes the President to use U.S. Armed Forces to enforce relevant United Nations Security Council resolutions and to "defend the national security of the United States against the continuing threat posed by Iraq.... " Although the 2002 AUMF has no sunset provision and Congress has not repealed it, it can be argued that after the establishment of a new Iraqi government, the restoration of full Iraqi sovereignty, and the U.S. withdrawal from Iraq, the 2002 AUMF no longer has force. The President has nonetheless stated that U.S. military action against the Islamic State in Iraq and Syria is authorized pursuant to the 2002 AUMF as well as the 2001 AUMF. Despite this reliance, the President included a provision to immediately repeal the 2002 AUMF in his February 11, 2015, draft authorization for use of military force against the Islamic State.

Uses of Force Pursuant to 2001 AUMF Authority

Acting under 2001 AUMF authority, U.S. Armed Forces began operations in Afghanistan on October 7, 2001, to neutralize the terrorist threat in that country by targeting Al Qaeda elements and infrastructure and removing the Taliban from power. The U.S. combat mission continued in Afghanistan until December 2014, including as part of NATO's International Security Assistance Force (ISAF). U.S. military action in Afghanistan continues in a reduced form in 2015.

In addition, since 2001, U.S. military action against terrorist groups has expanded to several other countries. Past comments from Obama Administration officials have indicated that military actions taken under the 2001 AUMF outside Afghanistan had nonetheless been limited in scope, at least until the current military campaign against the Islamic State. For example, in May 2014, an Administration official stated that 2001 AUMF-authorized military actions had included strikes in Yemen against Al Qaeda in the Arabian Peninsula (AQAP), considered either part of or associated with Al Qaeda, and operations to kill or capture Al Qaeda members in other countries, including Yemen and Somalia.[10] Drone strikes and other military operations in other countries, such as Pakistan and Libya, are also considered to be carried out under 2001 AUMF authority.

According to information provided at intervals by the executive branch in the 13-plus years since the 2001 AUMF was enacted, the United States has engaged in counterterrorism operations including the use of military force in a number of other countries. Since the 2001 AUMF's enactment, presidential notifications[11] to Congress have reported uses of military force, military deployments, and other activities in a number of countries and for a number of purposes, including to

- deploy U.S. Armed Forces and conduct military operations in several countries in a number of regions of the world, including most recently in Iraq and Syria against forces of the Islamic State and the Khorosan Group of Al Qaeda;
- counter generally the terrorist threat against the United States following September 11, 2001;
- engage terrorist groups "around the world";
- engage terrorist groups "on the high seas";
- detain individuals at Guantanamo Bay, Cuba, and to take other actions related to detainment decisions; and
- conduct trials of terrorist suspects in military commissions.[12]

These presidential notifications include language invoking either the authority or requirements of the 2001 AUMF, often in conjunction with the authorities and requirements of the War Powers Resolution (P.L. 93-148; 50 U.S.C. §§1541-1548), which requires the President to report military deployments and the introduction of U.S. Armed Forces into hostilities, with or without congressional authorization such as that provided in the 2001 AUMF. Some notifications state that certain military actions are taken pursuant to the President's authority as Commander in Chief and Chief Executive, including the authority to carry out the 2001 AUMF's provisions. While referencing the 2001 AUMF, such notifications often simply state that such reporting is "consistent with" the requirements of the 2001 AUMF, which directs the President to make reports periodically of U.S. military actions taken pursuant to the 2001 AUMF. Several notifications reference the 2001 AUMF at the beginning or end of a longer section on counterterrorism operations, which then lists a number of activities in several countries[13] without explaining each list item's connection to 2001 AUMF authority. As a result, it is often difficult to determine which military actions and which countries have been determined by the executive branch to fall within 2001 AUMF authority.

CURRENT EXECUTIVE BRANCH POLICY

President Obama and his Administration have publicly expressed support for possibly amending and eventually repealing the 2001 AUMF, in order to change the stance of the United States, as President Obama has termed it, "from a perpetual war-time footing."[14] According to Administration officials, the primary importance of the 2001 AUMF has been to authorize U.S. Armed Forces to enter into armed conflict with those who carried out or supported the September 11, 2001, terrorist attacks, namely Al Qaeda and the Taliban.[15] U.S. military operations against Al Qaeda and the Taliban occurred for more than a decade primarily in Afghanistan, and some U.S. Armed Forces currently remain there. Although the President announced the end of the U.S. military mission in Afghanistan in December 2014, he notified Congress in December 2014 that certain U.S. military operations against Al Qaeda in Afghanistan will continue pursuant to 2001 AUMF authority, and such operations have been reported in 2015.[16]

The United States and Afghanistan concluded a bilateral security agreement and status of forces agreement in late 2014, providing the basis under international law to remain in Afghanistan in a post-conflict role. The Obama Administration has stated that with the end of the U.S. combat mission in Afghanistan, it intends to work with Congress to either amend or repeal the 2001 AUMF. Administration officials have stated that any change to the 2001 AUMF should not, however, constrain the President's authority in a way that frustrates his ability to protect the United States from terrorist attacks and to meet U.S. counterterrorism objectives generally. The President has also maintained that he will oppose any attempt to legislate wider executive branch war-making authority. Instead, the Administration has proposed modernizing the counterterrorism authorities of the 2001 AUMF to precisely authorize the President to meet the current challenges posed by terrorist groups and networks around the world. Some Members of Congress have espoused this approach as well.

More recently, however, these stated Administration goals for the reform or repeal of the 2001 AUMF have been thrown into doubt by statements from the President and Administration officials in connection with U.S. military operations conducted against forces of the Islamic State and the Khorasan Group of Al Qaeda in Iraq and Syria. The President, in his August 2014 notifications to Congress, indicated that his powers as Commander in Chief and Chief Executive under Article II of the Constitution gave him authority to undertake deployments and airstrikes in Iraq against IS forces. The President's September 2014 notifications to Congress for airstrikes and other actions in Iraq and Syria, however, stated that the 2001 AUMF provides authorization[17] for certain U.S. military strikes against the Islamic State. Due to Al Qaeda's February 2014 disavowal of any remaining ties with the Islamic State, and the Islamic State's seeming lack of connection with the September 11, 2001, terrorist attacks, some experts have questioned whether the Islamic State can be targeted under the 2001 AUMF.[18] The Obama Administration has stated that the Islamic State can be targeted under the 2001 AUMF because its predecessor organization, Al Qaeda in Iraq, communicated and coordinated with Al Qaeda; the Islamic State currently has ties with Al Qaeda fighters and operatives; the Islamic State employs tactics similar to Al Qaeda; and the Islamic State, with its intentions of creating a new Islamic caliphate, is the "true inheritor of Osama bin Laden's legacy."[19] This interpretation seems to suggest that the Islamic State could be treated either as part of Al Qaeda that has splintered from the main group, or as an associate of Al Qaeda; under either interpretation, the Islamic State would arguably be targetable under the 2001 AUMF.

Prior to the wider military campaign against the Islamic State, the Obama Administration had stated that it will use limited force against individuals and groups outside Afghanistan under 2001 AUMF authority only when they are legally defined military targets that "pose a continuing, imminent threat to U.S. persons.... "[20] With regard to the current crisis in Iraq and Syria, the Administration has indicated that the Islamic State's threat to U.S. national security is one factor in the President's decision to conduct the current military campaign against the group. Although it is not clear whether the Administration is still adhering to this policy of limited force, the

Administration might have made a determination of a "continuing, imminent threat" from the Islamic State, thus plausibly placing the current military campaign within the limited scope of 2001 AUMF authority set out by the Administration prior to the Islamic State crisis. The ongoing, indefinite, large-scale military campaign against the Islamic State, outside the Afghanistan theater of operations, however, might be seen as an executive branch policy shift toward a more expansive interpretation of 2001 AUMF authority. Without a new authorization for use of military force specifically targeting the Islamic State, it seems the President would rely heavily on 2001 AUMF authority indefinitely to prosecute the military conflict against the group. Despite this, the President has continued to make statements confirming that Administration policy remains one of amending or repealing the 2001 AUMF, including in his February 11, 2015, letter to Congress accompanying his proposal for a new authorization for use of military force against the Islamic State.[21]

ISSUES CONCERNING THE CONTINUED USE OF THE 2001 AUMF

The executive branch's reliance on the 2001 AUMF has raised a number of concerns among some Members of Congress and policy analysts. These concerns relate to Congress's constitutional role in declaring and funding war, as well as several executive branch activities to counter terrorism that are perceived as problematic. In contrast, Obama Administration officials have testified that the legal framework for the current conflict against Al Qaeda and associated forces, which includes the 2001 AUMF, remains valid and effective in meeting the U.S. military's requirements for conducting counterterrorism operations, even as they state that they remain open to working with Congress to amend or repeal it.[22]

Constitutional Role of Congress in Authorizing the Use of Force

Some argue that Congress, since enacting the 2001 AUMF, has in some ways abdicated its role in directing the use of U.S. military force to counter terrorist threats. Congress, some contend, authorized the use of military force in haste during the initial reaction to the September 11 attacks, and has taken little legislative action since to tailor the use of such force to current circumstances. There are ongoing concerns that under the 2001 AUMF, especially regarding the use of unmanned aerial vehicles (UAVs), transparency in executive branch actions is lacking, and that Congress has neither voiced effective demands for information, nor asserted its role in decision-making through consultation and oversight. With the President's most recent reliance on 2001 AUMF authority to prosecute the military campaign against the Islamic State, calls to repeal the 2001 AUMF and terminate any newly enacted authority within three years seem to indicate that some in Congress are intent on using the legislative process to shape the course of ongoing counterterrorism and other military operations going forward.

Expanding Interpretation of 2001 AUMF Outside Original Scope

Observers assert that by its own terms, the 2001 AUMF over time has become obsolete, as it focuses directly on preventing the perpetrators of the September 11, 2001, attacks from carrying out further attacks against the United States, most of whom by now have been killed or captured.[23] It has been noted, however, that the 2001 AUMF remains central to the executive branch's justification for expanding efforts globally to counter terrorist threats, including continuing efforts against Al Qaeda. Administration officials assert that the 2001 AUMF is a key source of domestic legislative authority to conduct military operations against terrorist elements in any country where terrorist groups operate and plan to attack the United States or U.S. interests. The executive branch has targeted terrorist groups that are perceived by some to have only tenuous connections to those who perpetrated or supported the September 11, 2001, attacks.

In perhaps the most significant expansion of military action taken pursuant to 2001 AUMF authority, the President in September 2014 cited the statute as providing legal justification for U.S. military airstrikes and other operations against forces of the Islamic State and the Khorasan Group of Al Qaeda in Iraq and Syria. Many Members of Congress, however, claim that this is a new military campaign and requires a separate congressional authorization. Several proposals for a new authorization for use of military force targeting the Islamic State have been introduced, in both the 113th and 114th Congresses, and the President himself has proposed a new Islamic-State AUMF. None of these proposals have been enacted into law; the President continues to rely on 2001 AUMF and other authorities.

Broadening of Presidential Authority Through Multiple AUMFs

In addition to concerns about the perceived expanding scope of 2001 AUMF authority, maintaining the 2001 AUMF as current law might complicate congressional efforts to shape future authority granted to the President to use military force against other threats, such as the ongoing debate over authorizing military force against the Islamic State. Legislative proposals to authorize the use of military force against the Islamic State ("IS AUMF") have so far included a number of different provisions to limit the scope and duration of presidential authority to conduct military operations. Some are concerned that leaving the 2001 AUMF in place, with its broadly interpreted authorizing language, could neutralize any provisions in a new IS AUMF that purport to limit or otherwise shape the authority granted to the President. It could be argued that this sort of interpretation of congressionally granted authority, where multiple AUMFs are combined into one larger authority to conduct wider military operations, has already occurred, with the President relying on both 2001 and 2002 AUMF authority to conduct the current campaign against the Islamic State.

In an attempt to prevent this cumulative approach to multiple AUMF authorities, at least one IS AUMF proposal introduced in the 113th Congress stated that it constituted the sole authority to target the Islamic State militarily: "The provisions of this joint resolution pertaining to the authorization of use of force against the Islamic State of Iraq and the Levant shall supersede any preceding authorization for the use of military force."[24] This type of provision could prove less than effective, however, if Congress chooses to take no action to amend or repeal the 2001 AUMF's authority, especially in light of the President's position that the 2001 AUMF authorizes military action against the Islamic State.[25]

Controversial Activities and Policies Subsumed Under 2001 AUMF Authority

In addition to concerns about the 2001 AUMF's duration and scope, certain activities have also come under debate in connection with the 2001 AUMF.

Unmanned Aerial Vehicles

The Obama Administration's increased use of UAVs to strike terrorist elements abroad, yet away from the conventional battlefield, is one of the controversial activities for which the President has invoked 2001 AUMF authority. Critics of such drone strikes state that the practice is not sufficiently transparent, leaving the public and Congress without the information necessary to determine the propriety of the strikes through effective oversight. Moreover, critics argue that expanded UAV use targets far too many individuals, including low-level terrorist operatives as well as U.S. citizens abroad, raising constitutional due process concerns in the latter case. Collateral casualties and damage are also causes for concern. Because UAV strikes often are discrete incursions into foreign air space completed in short periods of time, and do not involve placing U.S. personnel in harm's way, some observers believe that the requirements of the War Powers Resolution for congressional consultation and authorization will become obsolete through the employment of this new remote warfare technology.

Detention of Terrorism Suspects and Individuals Designated as Enemy Combatants

Many observers object to the detention practices of the U.S. government regarding terrorism suspects and enemy combatants, including U.S. citizens, citing allegedly inhumane conditions at the Guantanamo facilities, the use of rendition to foreign governments, the indefinite nature of detention in many cases, the constitutional due process concerns such practices raise, and issues with the government's choices of military or civilian judicial venues for prosecution in different cases.[26]

Possible Domestic Use of Military Force Under the 2001 AUMF

Some government officials have indicated in recent years that U.S. military uses of force on U.S. territory could be authorized under the 2001 AUMF, sparking criticism. It is argued that because the 2001 AUMF does not contain explicit authorizing language for the use of force "within the United

States," it does not meet applicable legal requirements for using the U.S. military domestically under the Posse Comitatus Act, which states that the military cannot be used on U.S. territory to execute the law unless expressly authorized by the Constitution or an act of Congress.[27] Obama Administration officials have stated that they believe domestic uses of military force would be permitted only in the most extraordinary circumstances, and when such action is necessary to neutralize an identified domestically based threat to U.S. national security.[28] Although this eventuality remains unlikely, the issue of whether the 2001 AUMF or any other authorization for use of military force can be legitimately interpreted to authorize domestic military action without specific authorizing language could remain a concern.

ARGUMENTS TO MAINTAIN, REPEAL, OR AMEND/REPLACE THE 2001 AUMF

Some Members of Congress have supported legislative options to repeal, amend, or replace the 2001 AUMF, while others defend leaving it as is. Some of the key arguments being made in support of or against these options are considered below.

Maintaining the 2001 AUMF Status Quo

According to the Department of Defense, the 2001 AUMF provides authority to meet all U.S. military requirements to respond effectively and flexibly to terrorist threats globally, and allows the military to meet threats in conformity with domestic law and the international laws of war. Proponents of maintaining the 2001 AUMF as it stands state that it is important to ensuring the United States can continue to respond with force to terror threats. Repealing or narrowing the 2001 AUMF might remove legal authority to conduct certain counterterrorism efforts, and could undo authority to detain enemy combatants at Guantanamo Bay and elsewhere. Proponents of the status quo state that because the threat of terrorism will continue years into the future, the broad congressionally mandated authority in the 2001 AUMF is important to ensuring political legitimacy and the public's support for counterterrorism efforts.[29]

Some have argued, however, that counterterrorism operations will likely continue to expand in geographical and operational scope, and that Congress should take action to have a role in directing the course of using force against terrorist groups into the future. Others assert that maintaining the 2001 AUMF as is could provide an effective means of constraining presidential powers to conduct military operations against terrorist groups over time, for the very reason that its language is limited to those involved in the September 11, 2001, terrorist attacks, a list of groups and individuals that will arguably continue to dwindle as the numbers of those directly connected with the September 11, 2001, attacks diminishes. According to this view, if Congress were to leave the 2001 AUMF in place, uses of military force under 2001 AUMF authority will become increasingly constrained over time.

Repealing the 2001 AUMF Outright

Many argue that repealing the 2001 AUMF is necessary for a number of reasons:[30]

- the President announced in December 2014 that the military combat mission in Afghanistan had ended, and in other circumstances Congress has passed legislation formally ending war authority for other conflicts;
- the fight against terrorist groups has been improperly expanded and extended to the point that there are no effective restraints on presidential power in this area; and
- more emphasis should be placed on counterterrorism efforts that do not involve military force, such as disruption of terrorist financing and communications, economic development and assistance programs to populations vulnerable to terrorist influence, and law enforcement actions to arrest and prosecute terrorist suspects.

In addition, some argue that repeal would limit presidential authority to use force against terrorist groups to the powers contained in Article II of the Constitution and the international law of self-defense, standards that might in some cases be more restrictive than the authority in the 2001 AUMF. On the other hand, other observers claim that repeal would essentially ensure continued expansion of presidential Article II powers, as it would be expected that presidential uses of military force against terrorist groups would continue solely under Article II auspices. Some also oppose the repeal of the 2001 AUMF for reasons discussed in the prior section, including the belief that the 2001 AUMF is a necessary and appropriate measure to respond to ongoing terrorist threats.

Amending the 2001 AUMF or Replacing It with a New Authorization

Proposals to amend or replace the 2001 AUMF on the whole contemplate creating authority that is significantly more detailed than the general language of the 2001 AUMF, whether that detail restricts or expands presidential power to use force against terrorist elements globally.

Amending to Restrict Presidential Action

Proposals to restrict presidential power include setting out criteria that must be met to (1) introduce U.S. Armed Forces into another country; (2) conduct UAV strikes against terrorist targets, including U.S. citizens abroad; (3) detain and prosecute terrorist suspects; and (4) use military force in the United States. It has been suggested that a sunset clause should be included, as well as provisions to define the circumstances under which the threat of terrorist attack is neutralized and the authority to use force no longer adheres.[31] Similar to the argument to repeal the 2001 AUMF, leaving the President with more limited Article II powers, are proposals for a new authorization that merely reiterates that the President's only powers to use force to counter terrorism emanate from these limited Article II powers to defend against imminent attack on the United States, or to international law of self-defense. Others respond to these recommendations by warning that any restrictions placed on the President to prevent perceived overreach might restrict the U.S. military's flexibility in responding to emerging and changing terrorist threats in the future.[32]

Amending to Expand or Update Presidential Authorities

Alternatively, and not necessarily exclusive from proposals to restrict authority to use force, some Members recommend that Congress consider expanding or updating presidential authority to use force against terrorists.[33] These recommendations include updating language to detail new uses of force, such as UAVs and cyberwarfare, and specifying new terrorist groups that might not have ties to al Qaeda but still pose a threat to the United States.[34]

Some counter, however, that any update or expansion of authorities would further enshrine in law the idea of perpetual authorized war. They argue as well that new authorities might encourage Presidents to expand uses of force in undesirable ways, or to use armed force as a first resort, and that a new congressional imprimatur to continue the "war on terror" might produce a negative reaction from the international community, including U.S. allies. Any expansion of authorities specifically granting presidential power to conduct preventive war, it is asserted, would set an unfortunate precedent for an unfettered executive branch with the authority to kill anyone associated with terrorism, no matter how remote the threat to the United States; invade any country harboring terrorists who might someday attack the United States; and detain people indefinitely without due process of law.[35]

One set of recommendations[36] suggests providing a new authorization for the use of force against terrorist elements. This new authorization would set forth general legislative criteria for such uses of force, but it would also require the executive branch to identify targeted groups and geographic areas through an administrative process that includes congressional notification and waiting periods before becoming effective. This administrative process would operate much like the State Department's Foreign Terrorist Organization identification process.[37] Any such authorization would include specific criteria for using force, as well as precise definitions for key terms, such as "belligerent" and "imminent threat." Any such authorization would also require the executive branch to provide post-action reporting on any exercise of force under the authorization, and to assess a terrorist group's designation on a regular basis.

CURRENT LEGISLATIVE PROPOSALS CONCERNING THE 2001 AUMF

Over the past few Congresses, a number of legislative proposals contained provisions to sunset or repeal the 2001 AUMF, or to limit the use of appropriated funds to carry out the 2001 AUMF's provisions. These proposals were not enacted into law. With the advent of the Islamic State crisis and the U.S. military response, many proposals affecting the 2001 AUMF introduced late in the 113th Congress and early in the 114th Congress have been included in proposals for a new authorization for use of military force against the

Islamic State or are otherwise related to that crisis.[38] Current proposals specifically concerning the 2001 AUMF include the following:

- On February 2, 2015, Representative Adam Schiff introduced the Authorization for Use of Military Force Against ISIL Resolution (H.J.Res. 27). The resolution would repeal the 2001 AUMF three years after the resolution's enactment.
- On February 10, 2015, Representative Barbara Lee introduced the Comprehensive Solution to ISIL Resolution (H.J.Res. 30), which would repeal the 2001 AUMF as well as the 2002 AUMF. Repeal would become effective 60 days after enactment.
- Senator Ben Cardin introduced the Sunset of the 2001 Authorization for Use of Military Force Act (S. 526) on February 12, 2015. The bill would repeal the 2001 AUMF three years upon enactment.
- On March 4, 2015, Representative Barbara Lee introduced the Repeal of the Authorization for Use of Military Force (H.R. 1303), which would repeal the 2001 AUMF 180 days after enactment.

Past enacted legislation concerning the 2001 AUMF has generally confirmed executive branch claims of authority under the 2001 AUMF, such as provisions included in the 2006 and 2009 acts related to military commissions,[39] and the National Defense Authorization Act, Fiscal Year 2012 (NDAA 2012; P.L. 112-81). Section 1021 of the NDAA 2012 includes the term "associated forces" with regard to detentions of terrorist suspects; some claim that term has been effectively adopted into the authorities of the 2001 AUMF to justify broader authority for military action against loosely affiliated groups.

End Notes

[1] Jim Garamone, America Launches Strikes Against Al Qaeda, Taliban, American Forces Press Service, October 7, 2001, http://www.defense.gov/news/newsarticle.aspx?id=44680.

[2] Mark Mazzetti and Eric Schmitt, "In a Shift, Obama Extends U.S. Role in Afghan Combat," The New York Times, November 21, 2014, http://www.nytimes.com/2014/11/22/us/politics/in-secret-obama-extends-us-role-in-afghancombat.html.

[3] It is not clear whether the President's decision in 2014 to use military force against the Islamic State and the Khorasan Group in Iraq and Syria pursuant to the 2001 AUMF, among other authorities, occurred pursuant to a specific determination of an "imminent threat" to the United States.

[4] President Barack Obama, Letter from the President—Authorization for the Use of United States Armed Forces in connection with the Islamic State of Iraq and the Levant, February 11, 2015, http://www.whitehouse.gov/the-pressoffice/2015/02/11/letter-president-authorization-use-united-states-armed-forces-connection.

[5] Bold, italicized emphasis added. Senator Robert Byrd, reading President's proposal into the record in the Senate, Congressional Record, daily edition, October 1, 2001, pp. S9949-S9951.

[6] See "Expanding Interpretation of 2001 AUMF Outside Original Scope," below.

[7] See testimony of Mary McLeod and Stephen W. Preston, General Counsel, Department of Defense, before the Senate Committee on Foreign Relations, hearing on the Authorization for Use of Military Force, 113th Cong., 2nd sess., May 21, 2014, http://www.cq.com/doc/congressionaltranscripts-4481556?5.

[8] Available at http://www.whitehouse.gov/the-press-office/2014/09/23/letter-president-war-powers-resolutionregarding-iraq; http://www.whitehouse.gov/the-press-office/2014/09/23/letter-president-war-powers-resolutionregarding-syria.

[9] The President also relied on the Authorization for Use of Military Force Against Iraq Resolution of 2002 (2002 AUMF; P.L. 107-243) as authority for military action against the Islamic State.

[10] See Testimony of Stephen W. Preston, General Counsel, Department of Defense, before the Senate Committee on Foreign Relations, hearing on the Authorization for Use of Military Force, 113th Cong., 2nd sess., May 21, 2014, http://www.foreign.senate.gov/imo/media/doc/Preston_Testimony.pdf.

[11] Notifications of this type can be found in the Federal Register and the Compilation of Presidential Documents.

[12] After the Supreme Court found military commissions operating solely under 2001 AUMF authority to violate the Uniform Code of Military Justice (see Hamdan v. Rumsfeld, 548 U.S. 557 (2006)), Congress passed the Military Commissions Act of 2006 (P.L. 109-366) to continue trying terrorist suspects before these commissions. For more information, see CRS Report R41163, The Military Commissions Act of 2009 (MCA 2009): Overview and Legal Issues, by Jennifer K. Elsea.

[13] For example, President Bush's notification of September 20, 2002 mentions new or ongoing deployments to the Philippines, Georgia, and Yemen, in addition to Afghanistan and Guantanamo Bay, Cuba. The President stated that these actions had been taken according to his "constitutional authority to conduct U.S. foreign relations and as Commander in Chief and Chief Executive," but also states the actions were "consistent with P.L. 107-40." President George W. Bush, Letter to Congressional Leaders on the Deployment of Forces in Response to the Terrorist Attacks of September 11, 38 W.C.P.D. 1588, 1589 (September 20, 2002).

[14] President Barack Obama, Remarks by the President at the National Defense University, May 23, 2013, https://www.whitehouse.gov/the-press-office/2013/05/23/remarks-president-national-defense-university.

[15] Testimony of Mary McLeod and Stephen W. Preston, General Counsel, Department of Defense, before the Senate Committee on Foreign Relations, hearing on the Authorization for Use of Military Force, 113th Cong., 2nd sess., May 21, 2014, http://www.cq.com/doc/congressionaltranscripts-4481556?5.

[16] See Letter from President Barack Obama—Six Month Consolidated War Powers Resolution Report, December 11, 2014, http://www.whitehouse.gov/the-press-office/2014/12/11/letter-president-six -month-consolidated-war-powersresolution-report.

[17] As mentioned above, the President has also cited 2002 AUMF authority for these military actions.

[18] See, e.g., Robert Chesney, "The 2001 AUMF: From Associated Forces to (Disassociated) Successor Forces," Lawfare, September 10, 2014, http://www.lawfareblog.com/2014/09/the-2001-aumf-from-associated-forces-todisassociated-successor-forces/.

[19] White House, "Press Briefing by Press Secretary Josh Earnest," press release, September 11, 2014, http://www.whitehouse.gov/the-press-office/2014/09/11/press-briefing-press-secretary-josh-earnest-9112014.

[20] Testimony of Stephen W. Preston, General Counsel, Department of Defense, before the Senate Committee on Foreign Relations, hearing on the Authorization for Use of Military Force, 113th Cong., 2nd sess., May 21, 2014, http://www.foreign.senate.gov/ imo/media/doc/Preston_Testimony.pdf.

[21] President Barack Obama, Letter from the President—Authorization for the Use of United States Armed Forces in connection with the Islamic State of Iraq and the Levant, February 11, 2015, https://www.whitehouse.gov/the-pressoffice/2015/02/11/letter-president-authorization-use-united-states-armed-forces-connection.

[22] See statement of Robert Taylor, Acting General Counsel, Department of Defense, U.S. Congress, Senate Armed Services Committee, The Law of Armed Conflict, the Use of Military Force, and the 2001 Authorization for Use of Military Force, 113th Cong., 1st sess., May 16, 2013.

[23] See, e.g., Representative Adam Schiff, "Rep. Schiff Offers Amendment Sunsetting Authorization for Use of Military Force–'AUMF Never Intended to Authorize a War Without End'," press release, July 24, 2013, http://schiff.house.gov/ press-releases/rep-schiff-offers-amendment-sunsetting-authorization-for-use-of-military-force-aumf-never-intended-toauthorize-a-war-without-end/.

[24] See Sec. 6 of the Authorization for the Use of Military Force against the Islamic State of Iraq and the Levant (S.J.Res. 47).

[25] It should be noted that even with a limited authorization in a new IS AUMF and a repeal of the 2001 AUMF, the President could continue military operations against the Islamic State under other authority, including Article II authority as well as any legislation that continues to approve such military action through authorizing the use of appropriated funds for such operations. See CRS Report R41989, Congressional Authority to Limit Military Operations, by Jennifer K. Elsea, Michael John Garcia, and Thomas J. Nicola.

[26] For legal analysis of detention issues, see CRS Report R40139, Closing the Guantanamo Detention Center: Legal Issues, by Michael John Garcia et al.; CRS Report R42143, Wartime Detention Provisions in Recent Defense Authorization Legislation, by Jennifer K. Elsea and Michael John Garcia; and CRS Report R42337, Detention of U.S. Persons as Enemy Belligerents, by Jennifer K. Elsea.

[27] See CRS Report R42659, The Posse Comitatus Act and Related Matters: The Use of the Military to Execute Civilian Law, by Charles Doyle and Jennifer K. Elsea.

[28] Letter from Attorney General Eric Holder to Senator Rand Paul, March 4, 2013, available at http://www.cq.com/pdf/ govdoc-4231653.

[29] See Sara Sorcher, "Security Insiders: Narrow the Use-of-Force Act," National Journal, February 19, 2014, http://www.nationaljournal.com/defense/insiders-poll/security-insiders-narrow-the-use-of-force-act-20140219 (citing arguments of 29% of security experts in a survey argued for leaving the 2001 AUMF as is).

[30] See, e.g., "Repeal the Military Force Law," The New York Times, March 9, 2013. A number of legislative proposals introduced over the last several Congresses would have repealed the

2001 AUMF. For 2001 AUMF repeal proposals made in the 114th Congress, see "Current Legislative Proposals Concerning the 2001 AUMF," below.

[31] See Bill French and John Bradshaw, Ending the Endless War: An Incremental Approach to Repealing the 2001 AUMF, National Security Network, Washington, DC, August 2014, http://nsnetwork.org/report-ending-the-endlesswar/; Patricia Zengerle, "Amid new security threats, some in Congress look to update 9/11 law," Reuters, May 2, 2013, http://www.reuters.com/article/2013/05/02/us-usa-congress-counterterrorism-idUSBRE9 4105V20130 502.

[32] For analysis of the types of restrictions that might be included in a new AUMF targeting the Islamic State, and could similarly be included in amendments to the 2001 AUMF, see CRS Report R43760, A New Authorization for Use of Military Force Against the Islamic State: Issues and Current Proposals in Brief, by Matthew C. Weed.

[33] See, e.g., Andrew Cohen, "The Case for Congress Ending Its Authorization of the War on Terror," The Atlantic, June 10, 2013, http://www.theatlantic.com/politics/archive/ 2013/06/ the-case-for-congress-ending-its-authorization-of-thewar-on-terror/276699/.

[34] See Zengerle, op cit.

[35] See Rosa Brooks, "Mission Creep in the War on Terror," Foreign Policy, March 14, 2013, http://foreignpolicy.com/ 2013/03/14/mission-creep-in-the-war-on-terror/.

[36] Robert Chesney et al., A Statutory Framework for Next-Generation Terrorist Threats, Hoover Institution Task Force on National Security and Law essay, February 25, 2013.

[37] Section 219 of the Immigration and Nationality Act, as amended (P.L. 82-414; 8 U.S.C. §1189), sets out the process for designation of terrorist organizations.

[38] See CRS Report R43760, A New Authorization for Use of Military Force Against the Islamic State: Issues and Current Proposals in Brief, by Matthew C. Weed.

[39] Military Commissions Act of 2006 (P.L. 106-399); Military Commissions Act of 2009 (Title XVIII of the National Defense Authorization Act for Fiscal Year 2010, P.L. 111-84).

In: Authorization for Use of Military Force ... ISBN: : 978-1-63483-556-5
Editor: Tomas Mendoza

Chapter 3

THE "ISLAMIC STATE" CRISIS AND U.S. POLICY*

Christopher M. Blanchard, Carla E. Humud, Kenneth Katzman and Matthew C. Weed

SUMMARY

The Islamic State (IS, aka the Islamic State of Iraq and the Levant, ISIL/ISIS or the Arabic acronym *Daesh*) is a transnational Sunni Islamist insurgent and terrorist group that has seized areas of Iraq and Syria since 2013, threatening the wider region. There is debate over the degree to which the Islamic State organization may directly threaten U.S. homeland security or U.S. facilities and personnel in the region. Its advance threatens several U.S. regional partners. The forerunners of the Islamic State were part of the insurgency against U.S. and coalition forces in Iraq, and the organization has in the years since the 2011 U.S. withdrawal from Iraq expanded its control over significant areas of both Iraq and Syria. The Islamic State has thrived in the disaffected Sunni tribal areas of Iraq and taken control of some eastern provinces of Syria torn by that country's civil war. In 2014, Islamic State-led forces, supported by groups linked to ousted Iraqi President Saddam Hussein and some Sunni Arabs, advanced along the Tigris and Euphrates rivers in Iraq, seizing population centers including Mosul, one of Iraq's largest cities. Since

* This is an edited, reformatted and augmented version of a Congressional Research Service publication, No. R43612, dated June 11, 2015.

then, IS forces have massacred Syrian and Iraqi adversaries, including some civilians, often from ethnic or religious minorities, and murdered several hostages, including U.S. citizens. Islamic State attempts to make further gains continue. The group's tactics have drawn regional and international ire, and raised U.S. attention to Iraq's political problems and to the war in Syria.

On September 10, 2014, President Obama announced a series of actions intended to "degrade, and ultimately destroy" the Islamic State organization. The United States is leading a multilateral coalition that is undertaking direct military action; providing advice, training, and equipment for partner ground forces in Iraq and Syria; gathering and sharing intelligence; and using financial measures against the Islamic State. The objective of these measures is to progressively shrink the geographic and political space, manpower, and financial resources available to the Islamic State organization. U.S. officials refer to their strategy as "Iraq-first" and "ISIL-first," amid criticism by some in Congress that more attention should be paid to the civil war in Syria and more effort should be made to oust Syrian President Bashar al Asad.

As of mid-2015, observers continue to debate the success of U.S. and coalition efforts against the Islamic State. Some experts assert that coalition strikes and ground efforts by Iraqi security forces, Kurds, and predominantly Shiite Popular Mobilization Unit forces have shrunk the area of the Islamic State's control to some degree, but questions remain over whether operations by anti-IS forces and broader political arrangements will create conditions required for the group's lasting defeat. A May 2015 Islamic State offensive in Anbar Province and the fall of the provincial capital, Ramadi, raised some observers' doubts about Iraqi forces and U.S. policy even in the shorter term. U.S. efforts in Syria are less robust, and the Islamic State has both suffered losses to Kurds and other rebels and made gains against pro-Asad forces in fighting during 2015. President Obama has ruled out deploying ground combat forces to Iraq or Syria, but has not ruled out providing forward aircraft controllers, additional military advisors, new weapons, or other related ground-based military assets. Several U.S. regional partners apparently continue to seek to convince U.S. leaders of the necessity of ousting Asad. In December 2014, the 113th Congress provided new authorities and funds for efforts to combat the Islamic State organization in Syria and Iraq in the FY2015 national defense authorization (P.L. 113-291) and consolidated appropriations acts (P.L. 113-235). The 114th Congress is now considering the Administration's FY2016 appropriations requests, related appropriations and authorization legislation (H.R. 2685, H.R. 1735, and S. 1376), and proposals for the authorization for the use of military force against the Islamic State.

THE ISLAMIC STATE

The Islamic State (IS, aka the Islamic State of Iraq and the Levant, ISIL/ISIS) is a transnational Sunni Islamist insurgent and terrorist group that has expanded its control over areas of northwestern Iraq and northeastern Syria since 2013, threatening the security of both countries and drawing increased attention from the international community. The Islamic State has thrived in the disaffected Sunni Muslim-inhabited areas of Iraq and taken control of some Sunni-dominated provinces in eastern and central Syria. The Islamic State's tactics have drawn the ire of the international community, and raised new U.S. attention to Iraq's political problems and to the civil war in Syria.

The group also has sought to establish branches elsewhere in the Muslim world, and has attracted organized support in Egypt, Libya, Nigeria, Saudi Arabia, Yemen, and Afghanistan. It also appears to be inspiring attacks in Europe, and possibly in the United States.

In February 2015 congressional testimony, U.S. Director for National Intelligence James Clapper confirmed the intelligence community's earlier estimate that the Islamic State can muster "somewhere in the range between 20 and 32,000 fighters" but noted that there had been "substantial attrition" in its ranks since August 2014 and that the group had been turning to conscription in some areas.

As of March 2015, U.S. officials estimated that coalition air strikes and ground operations had killed thousands of IS personnel. However, thousands of recruits also reportedly have joined the organization since the start of coalition military operations, and U.S. officials have stated that uncertainty about casualty-to-replacement ratios for the Islamic State may persist until new information about IS recruiting and conscription, as well as flows of foreign fighters to the conflict zone, can be more fully reconciled with intelligence about ongoing battlefield attrition.[1]

Statements and media materials released by the Islamic State reflect an uncompromising, exclusionary worldview and a relentless ambition. Statements by IS leader Abu Bakr al Baghdadi and IS spokesman Abu Mohammed al Adnani feature sectarian calls for violence and identify Shiites, non-Muslims, and unsupportive Sunnis as enemies in the group's struggle to revive their vision of "the caliphate."

The group describes Iraqi Shiites derogatorily as "rejectionists" and "polytheists" and paints the Iraqi government as a puppet of Iran. Similar ire is aimed at Syrian Alawites and the Asad government, although some sources allege that operatives for the Islamic State and its antecedents benefitted from financial and security arrangements with Damascus that began during the 2003-2011 U.S. military presence in Iraq. The group's internal messages and activities emphasize service delivery and normalcy in a bid for support and recruits.

Although the Islamic State organization is considered a direct threat to U.S. interests in the Middle East, it is unclear whether it currently poses direct threats to U.S. homeland security.

A shooting attack by U.S. nationals in Texas in May 2015 was claimed by IS personnel overseas, but U.S. officials had not suggested any direct operational links between the attackers and the Islamic State organization as of early May. In November 2014, National Counterterrorism Center (NCTC) Director Nicholas Rasmussen said in congressional testimony that "the [ISIL] threat beyond the Middle East is real, although thus far limited in sophistication. However, if left unchecked, over time we can expect ISIL's capabilities to mature, and the threat to the United States homeland ultimately to increase."[2] In May 2015, a State Department official described the Islamic State as posing a formidable, enormous threat, and estimated that the group has attracted more than 22,000 foreign fighters from more than 100 countries.[3]

Al Baghdadi has threatened to attack the United States since 2012, and routinely describes the United States and its non-Muslim allies as "crusaders," while encouraging Islamic State supporters to attack U.S. persons, facilities, and interests overseas and at home.[4] The group's propaganda suggests that it welcomes the prospect of direct confrontation with the United States and its partners, viewing such conflict as a harbinger of apocalyptic confrontations described in some Islamic religious materials. In November 2014, Al Baghdadi argued the Islamic State would continue to expand and welcomed the potential introduction of Western ground forces, saying: "soon, the Jews and Crusaders will be forced to come down to the ground and send their ground forces to their deaths and destruction, by Allah's permission."[5] Some unconfirmed reports suggest Al Baghdadi has been injured, with uncertain implications for the leadership of the Islamic State organization. Nevertheless, in May 2015, an audio recording purportedly from Al Baghdadi praised the Islamic State's fighters, called for more Sunni support, and promised continued war against the group's enemies.

Background: The Roots of the Islamic State

The Islamic State's ideological and organizational roots lie in the forces built and led by the late Abu Musab al Zarqawi in Iraq from 2002 through 2006—*Tawhid wal Jihad* (Monotheism and Jihad) and Al Qaeda in the Land of the Two Rivers (aka Al Qaeda in Iraq, or AQ-I). Zarqawi took advantage of Sunni animosity toward U.S. forces and feelings of Sunni disenfranchisement at the hands of Shiites and Kurds to carry out a uniquely sectarian agenda that differed from Al Qaeda's in important ways. Following Zarqawi's death at the hands of U.S. forces in June 2006, AQ-I leaders repackaged the group as a coalition known as the Islamic State of Iraq (ISI). ISI lost its two top leaders in 2010 and was weakened, but not eliminated, by the time of the U.S. withdrawal in 2011. Under the leadership of Ibrahim Awad Ibrahim al Badri al Samarra'i (aka Abu Bakr al Baghdadi) and Taha Subhi Falaha (aka Abu Mohammed al Adnani)—both former U.S. detainees—ISI rebuilt its capabilities. By early 2013, the group was conducting dozens of deadly attacks a month inside Iraq. The precise nature of ISI's relationship to Al Qaeda leaders from 2006 onward is unclear.

In April 2013, Abu Bakr al Baghdadi announced his intent to merge his forces in Iraq and Syria with those of the Syria-based Jabhat al Nusra, under the name the Islamic State of Iraq and the Levant (ISIL/ISIS). Jabhat al Nusra and Al Qaeda leaders rejected the merger, underscoring growing tensions among Sunni extremists in the region. Al Qaeda leader Ayman al Zawahiri sought to remind IS leaders of previous pledges of loyalty to Al Qaeda made by deceased IS figures, but IS leaders rejected his claims, and Al Qaeda's general command issued a statement disavowing the Islamic State in early 2014. Islamic State leaders declared that their group "is not and has never been an offshoot of Al Qaeda,"[6] and said, given that they view themselves as a sovereign political entity, they have given leaders of the Al Qaeda organization deference rather than pledges of obedience. For an overview timeline, see Figure 4 below.

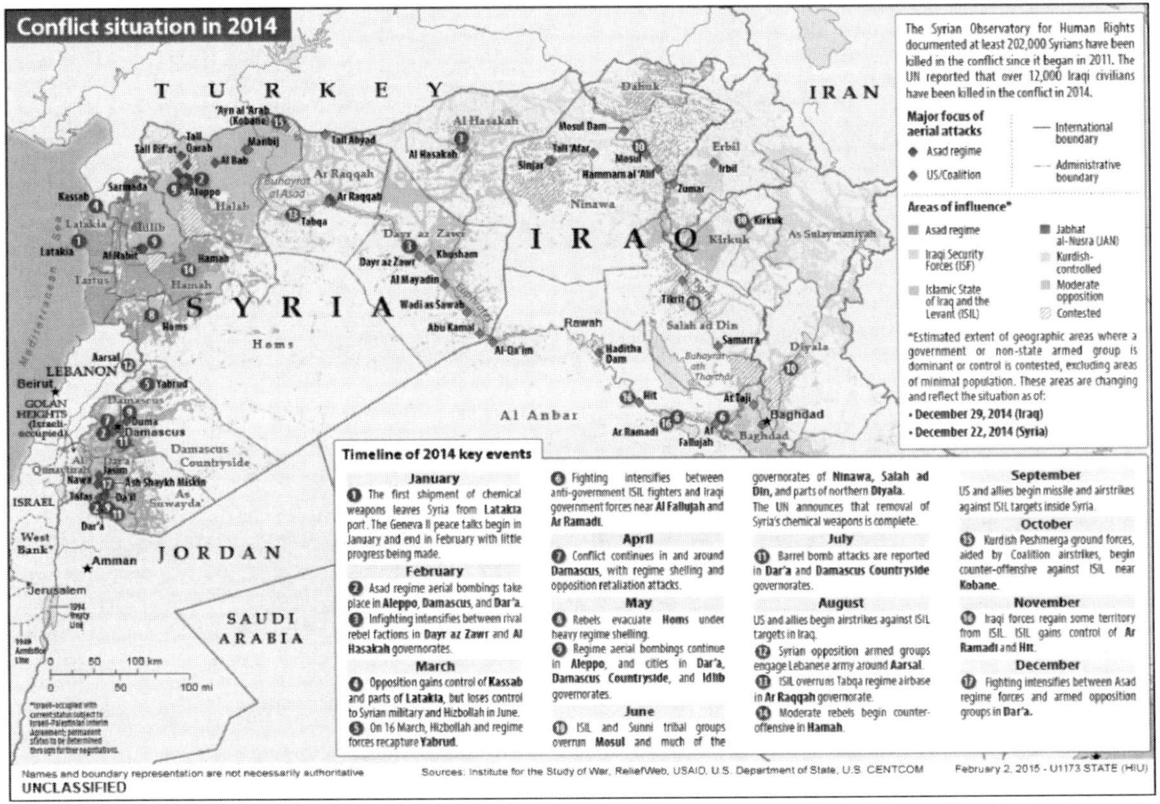

Source: U.S. State Department, Humanitarian Information Unit, Syria Conflict Without Borders: 2014 in Review, February 2, 2015.

Figure 1. Syria and Iraq: Conflict and Crisis in 201—Map and Timeline.

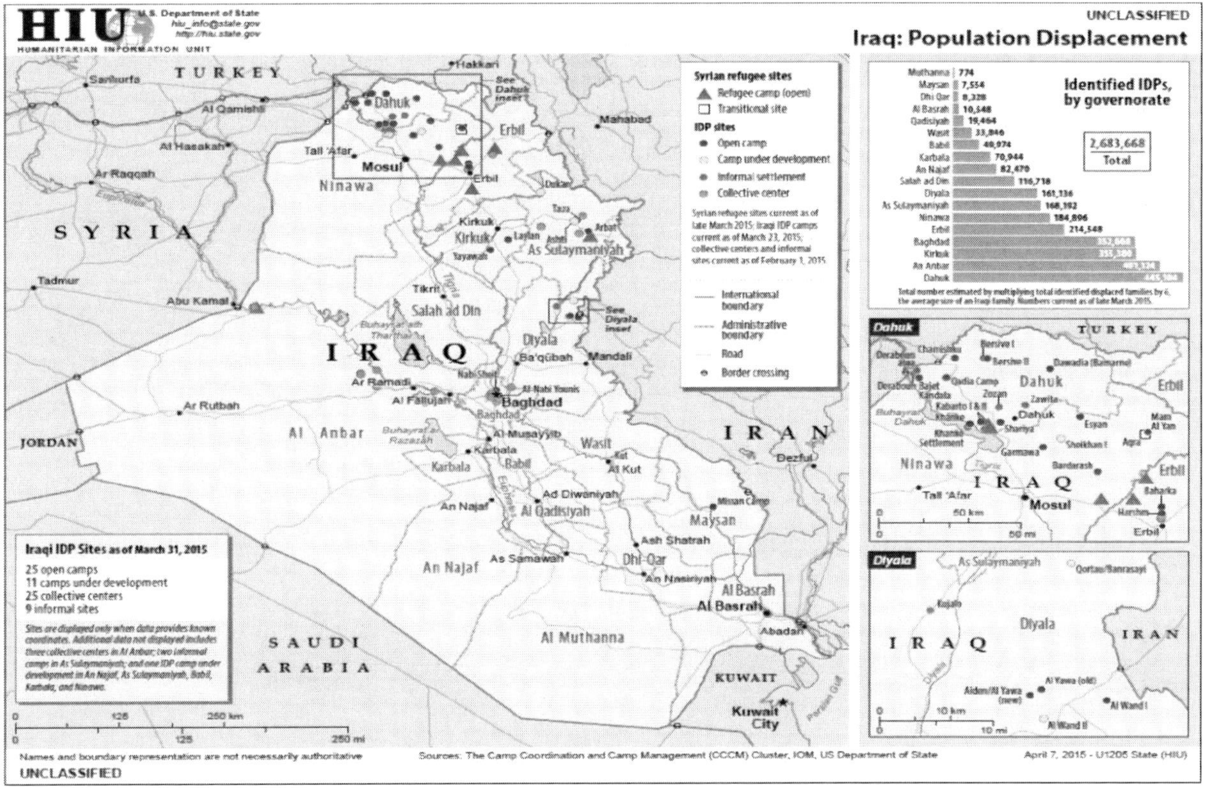

Source: U.S. State Department, Humanitarian Information Unit, Iraq: Population Displacement, April 10, 2015.

Figure 2. Iraq: Humanitarian Situation Map and Graphic.

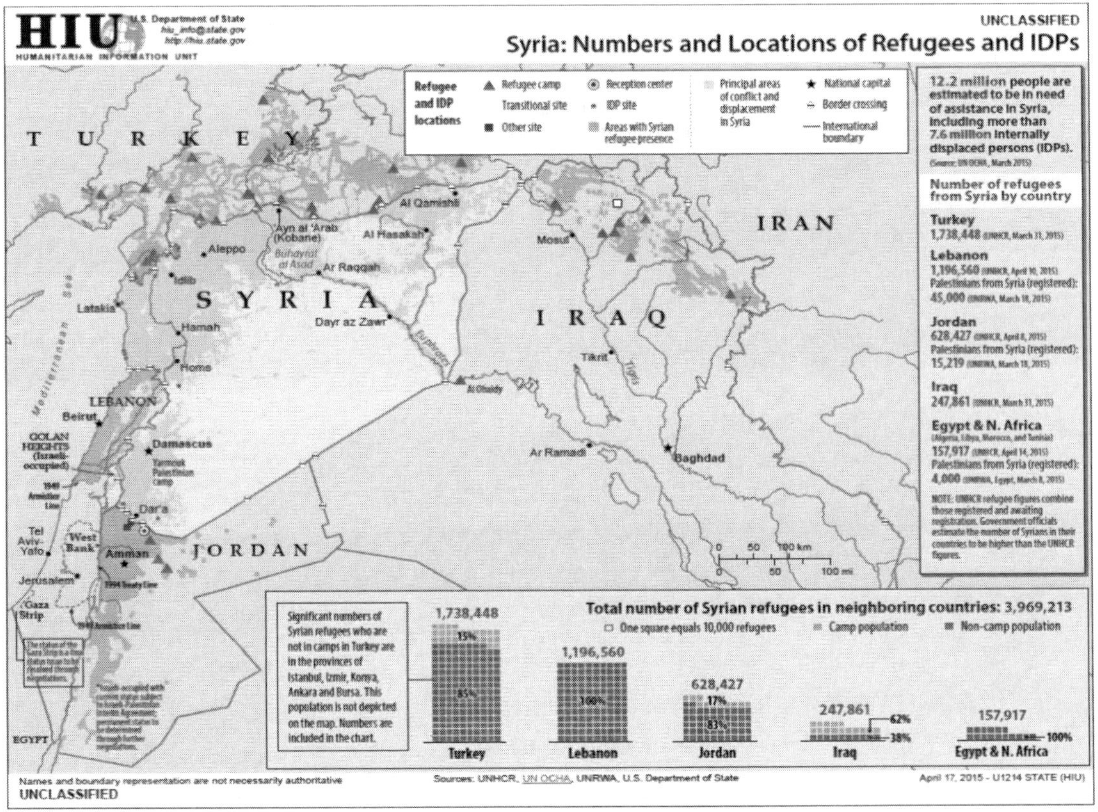

Source: U.S. State Department, Humanitarian Information Unit, Syria: Numbers and Locations of Refugees and IDPs, April 17, 2015.

Figure 3. Syria: Humanitarian Situation Map and Graphic.

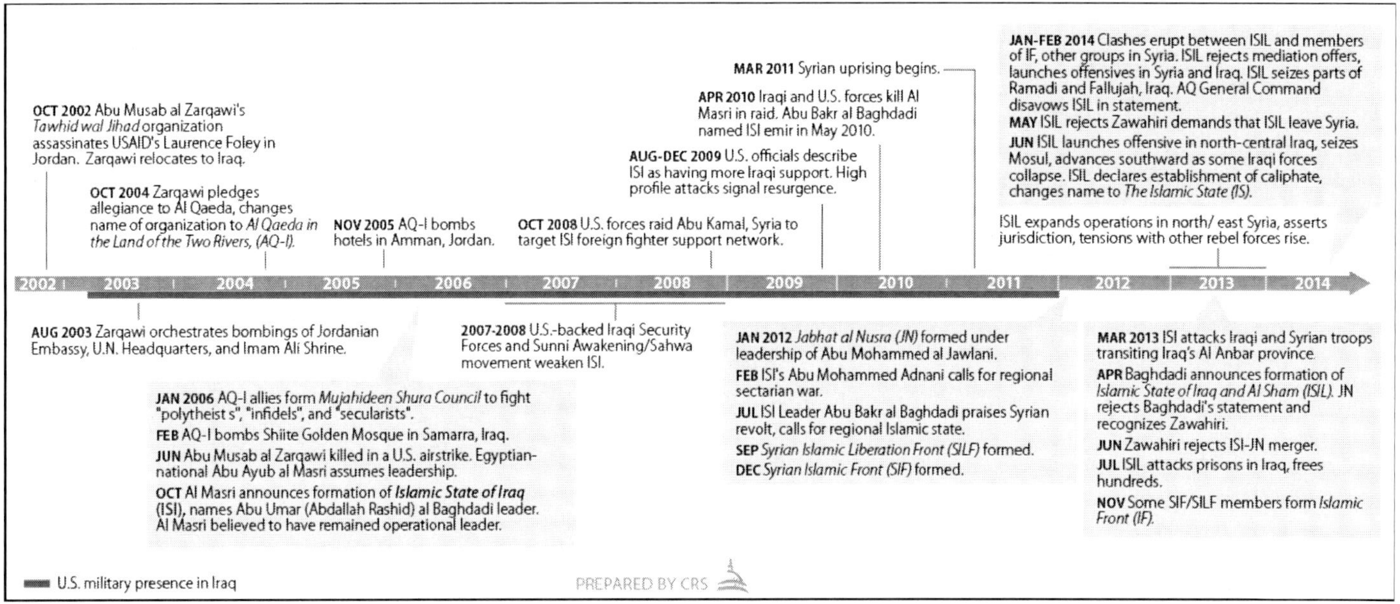

Source: Prepared by CRS using U.S. Government Open Source Center reporting and other open sources.

Figure 4. Timeline: The Roots of the Islamic State.

Overview

IS-Related Developments in Syria

Although U.S. intelligence officials told Congress in February 2015 "Worldwide Threat" testimony that the Asad regime held a military advantage in Syria's four-year-old civil war, various opposition forces and the Islamic State have scored a series of combat victories since March, increasing the pressure on pro-Asad forces on several fronts. Syrian observers and other international experts have credited apparent improvements in rebel coordination and reported financing and intelligence support from external third parties for the shift on the battlefield.[7] Leaders of powerful armed Islamist factions reportedly met in Turkey in early May to improve coordination among Islamist fighters with foreign support.[8]

On May 7, Chairman of the Joint Chiefs of Staff General Martin Dempsey acknowledged rebels' recent gains and told reporters that, "the situation is trending less favorably for the regime."[9] Subsequently, the Islamic State advanced southwestward and seized the central Syrian town of Tadmor and the adjacent antiquities of Palmyra, placing the country's central desert crossroads under its control and further isolating the few remaining pro-Asad forces in eastern Syria. Nevertheless, Syrian government forces retain a monopoly on air power and they and their foreign backers remain engaged in primarily defensive combat operations in several areas the country, amid reported manpower constraints.

The Islamic State organization has battled Syrian government, Kurdish, and opposition forces on a number of fronts in recent months. While the group has suffered some losses at the hands of Syrian Kurdish and Assyrian fighters in the northeast and other opposition groups in the south, it has not ceded additional large areas of territory in Syria following its ouster from the predominantly Kurdish border town of Kobane and its surroundings earlier this year. Islamic State personnel in northern Syria appealed for volunteers to support ongoing IS operations in Iraq in April 2015, and some reports have suggested for months that the provision of utilities, food, and water has become strained in some areas under IS control in Syria.[10]

The Islamic State's capture of Tadmor/Palmyra in May underscored the continuing threat posed by the group in Syria and its willingness and ability to conduct successful offensive ground operations there. The group's parallel seizure of the southeastern Syria/west-central Iraq border crossing at Al Tanf took the final border crossing from Syrian government hands other than crossings with Lebanon defended by Syrian military and Lebanese Hezbollah forces. Administration officials have not suggested that further opposition gains against pro-Asad forces would necessarily make efforts to combat the Islamic State organization easier, and President Obama and other leading U.S. officials have warned against the potential security and humanitarian consequences of a rapid collapse of the Asad government.[11] U.S. training efforts for vetted Syrians to combat IS forces and contribute to a negotiated settlement to the Syrian conflict began in May 2015 (see "U.S. Training and Equipment for Vetted Syrians" below), but the program is not expected to field combat-ready forces for months.

Northwest Syria

In late January 2015, Kurdish fighters backed by coalition airstrikes pushed IS forces out of the Kurdish town of Kobane in northern Syria. Fighting for control of the town, which borders Turkey, had been ongoing since September 2014.[12] Kurdish forces then pushed southward and westward to the banks of the Euphrates River, forcing IS personnel to retreat to strongholds across the river northeast of Aleppo. On March 6, pro-Kurdish sources reported that retreating IS fighters had destroyed the bridge spanning the Euphrates River near Jarabalus on the IS-controlled west bank to the Kurdish-controlled east bank just south of the Turkish border. A coalition airstrike on the town of Bir Mehli in late April targeted dozens of IS fighters, but some local activists claim that the strike killed more than 50 people, among them many civilians. As of May 6, a U.S. military spokesperson said the U.S. military had no indication that civilians had been killed in the strike.[13] Islamic State forces near Aleppo engage in regular fighting with Kurdish YPG and Arab opposition militias, who seek to expel IS personnel from the area.

Northeast and Eastern Syria

In the northeastern border province of Al Hasakah, Kurdish and Syrian government forces continue to clash with IS militants. Islamic State forces are conducting an offensive in the Khabour River Valley, with operations stretching from Ras al Ayn on the border with Turkey to Hasakah city. These areas are currently held by Kurdish Democratic Union Party Peoples' Protection Units (PYD/YPG, known for their anti-IS efforts in Kobane) as well as by Assyrian Christian fighters. While Islamic State forces reportedly have not made major gains in this area, the fighting in the region has likely prevented Kurdish fighters from re-taking territory from the Islamic State in other areas. Government and Islamic State forces have clashed in areas south of Qamishli. The fate of Assyrians seized by IS forces in late February northwest of Hasakah city remains unclear, although some hostages have been released. IS advances against the town of Tal Hamees northeast of Hasakah city near the Iraqi border and on Tal Tamr northwest of the city have been met with local counterattacks and new airstrikes by the U.S.-led anti-IS coalition. In mid-May, Kurdish fighters reported success in efforts to push IS fighters from the Tal Tamr region.

In the eastern border province of Dayr az Zawr, IS forces in the city of Al Miadin have come under attack by militants of unknown affiliation, leading the group to undertake a mass campaign of arrests targeting members of other opposition groups. Pro-Asad forces and IS forces remain locked in a struggle to control the city of Dayr az Zawr and nearby military facilities. IS fighters control much of the province and several neighborhoods in Dayr az Zawr city. The Islamic State's seizure of Tadmor/Palmyra severed the direct land link between areas held by pro-Asad forces in western Syria and military facilities to the west of Dayr az Zawr city.

Damascus and Southern Syria

Some observers suggest that the Islamic State is increasing its activities in central Syria and the Damascus suburbs, as a result of the increased battlefield pressure it faces from coalition strikes in Syria's northeast.[14] While IS expansion depends in part on securing defections from other rebel groups, the group has not succeeded in winning support from mainstream rebel coalitions and faces challenges in the south from the Al Qaeda-affiliated Jabhat al Nusra (Support Front) and other opposition groups. Social media reports in March suggested that IS forces had seized small areas 30 miles east of Homs and at least one town in the Damascus suburbs. In early April, IS forces took control of portions of the Yarmouk refugee camp in southwestern Damascus, home to a large Palestinian refugee population and an opposition stronghold that had long been isolated and bombarded by regime forces. Palestinian Islamists based in the camp resisted the IS advance, and other Islamist rebel groups such as the Ghouta (East Damascus)-based *Jaysh al Islam* (Army of Islam) blamed local Jabhat al Nusra members for enabling IS fighters to launch the assault. Also in April, IS forces launched attacks against government forces and the Khalkhalah military airport in Suwayda Province, home to most of Syria's Druze minority. Opposition groups including Jabhat al Nusra have attacked groups they accuse of supporting IS in several areas of the south in recent weeks, most notably in Quneitra province where Nusra forces defeated a group known as *Jaysh al Jihad* (Army of Jihad).

IS-Related Developments in Iraq

As of April 2015, Iraqi counteroffensives and coalition airstrikes had succeeded in pushing Islamic State (IS) forces back from the maximum extent of their June-August 2014 gains (see **Figure 5** below). Nevertheless, IS fighters have continued to advance on some battlefronts across the country, and, in May 2015, placed new pressure on Iraqi forces across Anbar Province and near the Baiji oil refinery complex in north-central Salahuddin Province. The Islamic State's April-May 2015 IS offensive against Ramadi—Anbar's provincial capital—succeeded in breaking the Iraqi military's long resistance in the city and forced more than 100,000 Iraqis from their homes. The withdrawal of Iraqi Security Forces from Ramadi cast some doubt on the success of Iraqi, coalition, and U.S. efforts to date in preparing and equipping Iraqi forces to resist and reverse IS advances. A State Department official described the situation as "extremely serious,"[15] but, like other U.S. officials, expressed some confidence in the willingness and ability of Iraqi leaders to respond and make changes in policy. The terms and outcome of an ongoing counteroffensive in Anbar Province by various Iraqi forces remain to be seen. For the moment, the fighting in Anbar Province has overshadowed planning for operations to retake northwestern Nineveh Province, and its capital Mosul, which had been under discussion earlier in 2015. Recent visits to Washington, DC, by Iraqi Prime Minister Haider al Abadi, Kurdistan Regional Government (KRG) President Masoud Barzani, and some Iraqi Sunni leaders focused on anti-IS operations, as well as proposals and requests by the Iraqi government and Kurdish and some Sunni leaders for U.S. support. Administration officials continue to emphasize the importance of Iraq's national government taking the lead in the fight against the Islamic State and U.S. diplomats and military officers remain engaged in efforts to encourage Iraqis to make necessary policy changes and provide needed support.

Iraqi Forces Retake Tikrit, Controversies Emerge

The fall of Ramadi overshadowed an earlier success, the March 2015 recapture of the city of Tikrit in Salahuddin Province from the Islamic State organization. After weeks of fierce fighting, Iraqi military and primarily Shiite Popular Mobilization Force militia units bested IS forces. U.S. military air support coincided with the decisive final push in the campaign: Prime Minister Abadi requested U.S. support after Iraqi forces and Iranian-advised militia groups were halted by IS resistance and improvised explosive devices. Iraqi and regional media reports suggest that some pro-Iranian militia forces protested the Abadi government's request for U.S. assistance and U.S. involvement, and they withdrew from the fighting. These reports also allege that a division is emerging between religiously motivated, pro-Iranian Shiite militia forces and a more nationalist Shiite militia coalition.[16]

In the wake of the victory in Tikrit, reports of looting and abuses by some Popular Mobilization units drew severe criticism from Iraqis and certain international observers—although some reports suggested that such abuses were far fewer than in previous victories by Iraqi government and Shia militia forces. Still, Abadi ordered security forces to "confront any acts of sabotage practiced by the gangs that want to do harm to the heroism achieved by our brave fighters and the volunteers of the Popular Mobilization."[17] Days later, he and the Council of Ministers placed all Popular Mobilization units under his direct command. The effectiveness of Abadi's attempted reorganization remains to be seen. Some IS-related resistance reportedly remained in Tikrit and the surrounding areas, where Iraqi forces continue to engage in fighting as of late May 2015.

Fall of Ramadi Derails Planned Anbar Offensive, Counterattack Launched

On the heels of Iraqi forces' recapture of Tikrit, Abadi visited Anbar Province and announced that the Iraqi military would work with local tribal forces and select Popular Mobilization units to eject IS fighters from their strongholds in the province. Since 2014, IS forces had held more populated areas in the province than Iraqi forces, and the campaign in the province looked likely to be protracted and difficult. After Abadi visited the province and announced the approval of the sale of light and medium weaponry to tribally organized forces, IS fighters seized control of towns on the outskirts of the provincial capital of Ramadi and later launched a fierce assault that led Iraqi security forces to withdraw from the city. Tens of thousands of Sunni civilians fled eastward and southward toward Baghdad, and local Sunni officials approved the deployment of predominantly Shiite Popular Mobilization Unit forces to the area in a bid to halt the IS advance. Local press reports prior to Ramadi's fall suggested that IS fighters had moved to the area from IS-held regions of northern Iraq as well as from Syria, using the IS-controlled Syrian-Iraqi border crossing at Al Qaim/Albu Kamal. Some observers argue that IS leaders may have launched the assault to preempt emerging Iraqi preparations to retake the province using local fighters. Others disagree and note the Islamic State's continual efforts to take Ramadi over a period of 18 months.

Ramadi's fall and the subsequent urgency for the ISF of defensive measures and a counterattack have introduced new challenges for Iraqi leaders who were already attempting to arm, train, manage, and supply a diverse blend of forces over a wide geographic area. Iraqi army forces, tribal forces, and some Popular Mobilization forces were reported to be part of the plans for operations in Al Anbar prior to the Ramadi withdrawal. According to the State Department, Iraqi leaders have approved a number of changes designed to facilitate the recapture of Anbar Province since Ramadi's fall, including "mobilizing tribal fighters in Anbar, with a streamlined delivery mechanism for weapons"; reconstituting the Anbar-based 7th Iraqi Army Division and provincial police; engagement with governors and local leaders on decentralization; and new efforts to secure approval for a long-awaited national guard law.[18] The terms of these new efforts are still emerging and their success is not guaranteed. As discussed below, President Obama has announced the deployment of 450 additional U.S. military personnel to augment training efforts in Anbar province.

In the interim, initial operations to halt the Islamic State's advance and retake the town prominently feature predominantly Shiite Popular Mobilization Unit forces, which may prove to be a source of tension in the months ahead. In an April interview, leader of the Sunni Al Dulaym tribe Majid al Ali al Suleiman said

> Al Anbar and its tribes do not need the Popular Mobilization for two main reasons. The first is that Al Anbar does not need men, but needs weapons. The second reason is that we do not want to enter into problems and disputes with our brothers from the Shiites in the south. ... the Iraqi Army, given that it brings together all Iraqis, is welcome and no one can stand in its face anywhere in Iraq. As for the other names [militias], they are still subject to debate and disagreement.[19]

More broadly, the fall of Ramadi has raised questions about the efficacy of U.S. strategy. Some interpreted that battle as evidence that there has not been a major shift by Iraqi Sunni Arabs to support the Iraqi government. Others attributed the defeat to U.S. insistence on supporting only the ISF, and not certain Shiite militias among the Popular Mobilization Units that now comprise a large part of Iraq's overall combat capability against the Islamic State. Some Iraqi commentators suggested that the loss was caused by insufficient supplies of U.S. weapons and an airstrike strategy that insists on minimizing any incidental civilian casualties. Some U.S. military officials asserted that the ISF is poorly commanded, and that command confusion largely caused the loss of Ramadi. Other U.S. officials emphasized the ferocity of the tactics used by IS forces in the assault, including the reported use of dozens of high-powered suicide bombs delivered in armored vehicles. U.S. officials announced plans to speed the delivery of anti-tank weapons to combat IS armored vehicle bombs like those used in the Ramadi assault.[20]

Source: U.S. Department of Defense, April 10, 2015. Author of note in map is Department of Defense.

Figure 5. U.S. Department of Defense Map: Syria and Iraq—As of April 10, 2015.

Some experts said the interpretation of the Ramadi loss has been overstated and does not affect the trajectory of the mission.[21] In a briefing days before Ramadi's fall, U.S. military officers described a range of defensive measures and tactics taken by IS fighters in recent months as evidence of their overall posture amid periodic, limited, but dangerous offensive operations.[22] After Ramadi fell, a senior State Department official acknowledged the development as a serious setback, but stated that Iraqis were not "panicking" and that the withdrawal of the ISF from the city rather than their defeat in place provided an opportunity to reconstitute the forces and send them back into the fight.[23] The White House has identified a "combination of [a] multi-sectarian force under the command and control of the Iraqi central government backed by military coalition air power" as a viable model for retaking Ramadi and for future operations more broadly.[24]

Plans for Joint Mosul Operations with Kurdish Forces under Consideration

Prime Minister Abadi visited Erbil, the capital of the autonomous Kurdish Regional Government (KRG), in early April 2015 for consultations with KRG President Masoud Barzani. Reportedly, the two leaders discussed potential joint operations between Iraqi armed forces and Kurdish *peshmerga* and agreed upon the importance of close coordination. The timing and scope of anti-IS operations in Nineveh Province remain under discussion, with Kurdish forces continuing to engage IS adversaries on several fronts, including in the areas west of Mosul, near Sinjar. As noted above, the apparent urgency of operations in Anbar Province appears likely to delay operations against Mosul considerably. On May 20, a State Department official said that "Mosul will happen when it's ready. So it could be some time from now, but we're focused on Anbar."[25]

During a May 2015 visit to Washington, DC, KRG President Barzani stated that he had been given "assurances" by his U.S. interlocutors that weaponry and supplies would be provided to Kurdish peshmerga forces as part of the "Iraqi national defense system" in the coming months (see "Support for Kurdish Forces" below).[26] Congress continues to debate the proper mechanisms for the provision of U.S. assistance to Kurdish forces, with several pieces of proposed legislation calling for the direct delivery of assistance, and Administration and some Iraqi leaders warning that directly provided U.S. assistance could increase ethnic and sectarian tension in Iraq (see "Defining the Way Forward in Iraq" and "FY2016 Budget Requests for Foreign Operations and Defense" below).

U.S. Strategy to Combat the Islamic State Organization in Iraq and Syria

At President Obama's direction, elements of the U.S. government are leading a multilateral coalition that seeks to "degrade and ultimately destroy" the Islamic State organization by progressively reducing the geographic and political space, manpower, and financial resources available to it.[27] The United States and other members of the coalition are undertaking various measures, including direct military action, support for Iraqi and Syrian partner ground forces, intelligence gathering and sharing, and efforts to restrict flows of foreign fighters and disrupt the Islamic State's finances.[28] Administration officials have described U.S. policy in Syria and Iraq as being driven by "ISIL-first" and "Iraq-first" approaches. Administration officials have identified areas where they believe progress has been made in implementing U.S. strategy to date, but have stated clearly that it may take months, and in some cases years to achieve the full range of U.S. objectives. In Iraq, the Administration emphasizes the importance of providing support to multi-sectarian security forces under central government command and the preservation of Iraq's political and territorial unity pursuant to its constitution.

President Obama said on November 5, 2014, that the United States seeks to isolate and reduce the areas where the Islamic State can operate in Syria in support of the top U.S. priority of rolling back IS gains in Iraq. To date, the Syrian government and Syrian military have fought the Islamic State in some areas but are not active partners in U.S. or coalition efforts against IS fighters inside Syria. In September 2014, U.S. officials reportedly warned the Syrian government of impending strikes on Syrian territory, but President Obama has said that the United States will not coordinate its actions in Syria with the Asad regime, which he said "terrorizes its own people" and "will never regain the legitimacy it has lost."[29] In January 2015, President Asad said in an interview that he was open to cooperation with coalition forces but suggested that Syria had not granted "permission" for the ongoing coalition military strikes in Syria.[30]

U.S. strategy seeks a negotiated settlement to the conflict in Syria and argues that President Asad and some of his supporters must leave office as part of such a settlement. Congress and the Administration have provided nonlethal aid and reportedly provided lethal support in the form of weaponry and funding to some opposition groups in Syria. A new U.S. training program for Syrian fighters to combat the Islamic State has begun in earnest, and mirrors

U.S. military training and support programs for Iraqi and Kurdish fighters. By all accounts, Syrian opposition forces remain divided in their goals and varied in their cohesiveness and capabilities.

At the same time, some experts have taken note of setbacks for the strategy and argue that the U.S. goal should change to one of "containment" of the Islamic State in Iraq and Syria, rather than outright defeat.[31] Those who take this view maintain that defeating the Islamic State is likely beyond U.S. and partner capabilities in the context of resources and risks that the United States and partner countries are willing to bear. Advocates for a containment strategy tend to assess that linkage between Islamic State success in the Middle East region and any direct terrorist threat to the U.S. homeland is tenuous. Opponents of this view contend that allowing the Islamic State to continue to exist risks perpetuating the threat to U.S. partners and interests and may provide the group with an opportunity to focus on attacking the United States, whether at home or abroad.

In support of his current policy, President Obama has requested funds from Congress for military operations and train and equip programs for U.S. partners in Iraq and Syria in FY2016 (see "FY2016 Budget Requests for Foreign Operations and Defense" below).

Key U.S. Personnel

Retired General John Allen serves as Special Presidential Envoy for the Global Coalition to Counter ISIL, and Brett McGurk, Deputy Assistant Secretary of State for Near Eastern Affairs (Iraq and Iran), serves as General Allen's deputy senior envoy with the rank of Ambassador. U.S. military operations as part of the anti-IS strategy have been termed "Operation Inherent Resolve." U.S. Central Command (CENTCOM) Commander General Lloyd Austin is the lead U.S. officer with respect to military operations against the Islamic State and other extremists in Iraq and Syria. Daniel Rubenstein serves as U.S. Special Envoy for Syria. Ambassador Thomas Krajeski serves as the State Department Bureau of Counterterrorism Senior Advisor for Partner Engagement on Syria Foreign Fighters. The Department of the Treasury's Office of Terrorism and Financial Intelligence leads efforts to disrupt IS finances. Major General Michael Nagata, Commander, Special Operations Command—Central, is leading the new congressionally authorized program to train and equip vetted members of Syria's opposition and other vetted Syrians.

Military Strikes against IS Targets

U.S. and coalition forces have used combat aircraft, armed unmanned aerial vehicles, and sea-launched cruise missiles to conduct more than 3,700 strikes in Iraq since August 8, 2014, and in Syria since September 22, 2014.[32] The stated objectives of U.S. strikes have evolved as circumstances have changed and some goals have been achieved: The initial focus was on stopping the advance of Islamic State forces and reducing threats to American personnel and religious minorities in northern Iraq; now it is supporting defensive and offensive military operations by Iraqi military and Kurdish forces and weakening the Islamic State organization's ability to support its operations in Iraq from its bases inside Syria. Other U.S. strikes have targeted individuals and locations associated with what U.S. officials describe as "the Khorasan Group," a reputed affiliate of Al Qaeda's central leadership still based in Pakistan and that reportedly has engaged in preparations for transnational terrorist attacks.[33]

President Obama has stated that he does not believe the introduction of large-scale U.S. ground forces for combat operations is necessary in order to achieve U.S. objectives. Rather, he has stated that U.S. efforts to reverse Islamic State gains on the ground will pair continued airstrikes with expanded efforts to advise and strengthen local Iraqi and Syrian partner forces. Some U.S. military officials have indicated that they are prepared to recommend the introduction of some ground forces if they believe such forces are required to achieve U.S. objectives.[34] Some Members of Congress have suggested U.S. military ground forces may be required to achieve short-term objectives and protect long-term national security interests. In March 2015 congressional testimony, some U.S. military officials suggested that U.S. and coalition air operations in Iraq and Syria could continue for three or more years.[35] In late May, White House spokesman Josh Earnest said:

> We have seen what happens when the United States tries to insert a large military contingent to try to solve this problem for the Iraqi people. Because of the bravery and courage and service of—and skill of the American military, that can work for a short period of time. But for enduring, sustainable results, we're going to need to see the Iraqi people, the Iraqi government and the Iraqi security forces step up and take responsibility for the security situation in their own country. And that's going to mean training Iraqi security forces and that's a training process that can't be done in a week. That's not a seven-day training force. This is going to require a more sustained commitment.[36]

"Train and Equip" Assistance

Iraqi Security Forces

As of June 2015, approximately 3,100 U.S. military personnel have deployed to the Iraq theater of operations to advise and train Iraqi forces, gather intelligence on the Islamic State, and secure U.S. personnel and facilities. Of the total, about two-thirds are advisers and trainers for the Iraqi Security Forces (ISF) and the peshmerga, and the rest support these forces and provide protection for U.S. civilian and military personnel in country.[37] Coalition partners also have pledged and begun deploying about 1,500 advisers and trainers for the ISF. On June 10, President Obama announced the deployment of an additional 450 military personnel to expedite training of Iraqi forces at the Taqqadum military base near Habbaniyah in Anbar Province.[38]

U.S. and coalition personnel are implementing joint Iraqi-coalition plans for the training of 12 Iraqi brigades (nine Iraqi Security Force [ISF] brigades and three Kurdish *peshmerga* brigades—a total of about 25,000 personnel). According to Major General Paul Funk, commander of Coalition Joint Forces Land Component Command-Iraq and the 1st Infantry Division, U.S. forces working at five capacity building sites had trained two Iraqi brigades as of early April and another three were "in various stages of readiness."[39] In mid-April, the Obama Administration reported that 6,500 ISF personnel, "including *peshmerga*," had completed instruction and "more than 4,900" were then in training.[40] Training is expected to continue over a period of about 8 to 10 months.

The U.S. and partner deployments are intended to address severe weaknesses in Iraq's ground forces. After undertaking an assessment of Iraqi military forces in 2014, U.S. advisers concluded that only about half of all Iraqi Security Forces (ISF) units were sufficiently capable for U.S. advisers to help them regain captured territory through the provision of further targeted advisory assistance.[41] The definition of "capable," according to U.S. officials, included whether an ISF unit integrates both Sunni and Shiite personnel. Some private assessments by nongovernment observers argued that even fewer ISF units were capable of reversing the Islamic State gains, and underscored the continuing role of Shiite militia groups in defending Iraqi-government held-territory and conducting offensive operations against IS forces.

U.S. military personnel in Iraq are currently not tasked with providing advisory or training support to Iraqi personnel in combat settings or with engaging directly in combat against hostile entities other than for force protection purposes. Chairman of the Joint Chiefs of Staff Martin Dempsey acknowledged in November 2014 that as the campaign against the Islamic State progresses and more complex operations are required by Iraqi Security Forces, he could recommend that U.S. personnel accompany Iraqi forces.[42]

Congress authorized and provided $1.6 billion in funding for the U.S. training efforts in Iraq in the FY2015 National Defense Authorization Act (NDAA, H.R. 3979, P.L. 113-291) and FY2015 appropriations act (H.R. 83, P.L. 113-235). The funding provision (Iraq Train and Equip Fund in Division C of P.L. 113-235) stipulates that 40% of the requested U.S. train and equip funds is not eligible to be expended unless foreign contributions equal to 40% of the $1.618 billion are contributed (of which half that contributed amount would come from the Iraqi government). The FY2015 National Defense Authorization Act (NDAA, Section 1236 of P.L. 113-291) includes this cost-sharing provision, and also limits the availability of funds for the newly authorized Iraq training program to 25% until the Administration submits required program and strategy reports to Congress. It also requires 90-day progress reporting.

Under the FY2015 NDAA, the Secretary of Defense, in coordination with the Secretary of State, is authorized:

> to provide assistance, including training, equipment, logistics support, supplies, and services, stipends, facility and infrastructure repair and renovation, and sustainment, to military and other security forces of or associated with the Government of Iraq, including Kurdish and tribal security forces or other local security forces, with a national security mission, through December 31, 2016, for the following purposes:
>
> (1) Defending Iraq, its people, allies, and partner nations from the threat posed by the Islamic State of Iraq and the Levant (ISIL) and groups supporting ISIL.
>
> (2) Securing the territory of Iraq.

The Administration's FY2016 Defense appropriations request seeks a further $715 million in U.S. funding for the Iraq training program. The House-passed version of the FY2016 National Defense Authorization Act (Section 1223 of H.R. 1735) would authorize the appropriation of $715 million in Overseas Contingency Operations (OCO) funding for security assistance to Iraqi security forces, including the Kurdish *peshmerga*; Sunni tribal security forces with a national security mission; and a proposed "Iraqi Sunni National Guard." Prime Minister Abadi and some other leading Iraqis have criticized congressional proposals to authorize the provision of U.S. assistance directly to certain forces other than the ISF (see "Iraqi Kurdish and Sunni Arab Forces," "Defining the Way Forward in Iraq," and "FY2016 Budget Requests for Foreign Operations and Defense" below).

Foreign Military Sales and Arms Transfers

In conjunction with expanded training efforts, the United States also has undertaken new efforts to equip existing Iraqi forces. Since the Islamic State-led capture of Mosul in June 2014, the United States has proposed sales of over 5,000 additional HELLFIRE air-to-surface missiles[43] to Baghdad and has delivered "the equivalent of roughly 5-6 brigades' worth of individual soldier weapons and equipment."[44] Deliveries of U.S.-made F-16s, first proposed for purchase by Iraq in 2011,[45] remain in their early stages, with Iraqi pilots "in the training pipeline." Deliveries of 250 U.S.-donated Mine Resistant Armor Protected Vehicles (MRAPs) were completed in early 2015, with 50 more planned as of April 2015.[46] In December 2014, U.S. officials also proposed sales to Iraq that may be worth nearly $3 billion for 1,000 M1151AI Up-Armored High Mobility Multi-Purpose Wheeled Vehicles (HMMWVs) and 175 M1A1 tanks with spare parts, communications, and ammunition.[47] Press reports suggest that during his April 2015 visit to Washington, DC, Prime Minister Abadi sought U.S. approval for the delivery of Apache attack helicopters first proposed for sale and lease in 2014[48] and unmanned aerial vehicles. In the wake of the fall of Ramadi and the Islamic State's reported mass use of armored vehicle bombs there, U.S. officials announced plans to speed the delivery of 2,000 unguided AT-4 anti-tank weapons to Iraqi forces.[49]

The Senate Armed Services Committee-reported version of the FY2016 NDAA (Section 1225 of S. 1376) would prohibit the provision of further assistance to Iraq "unless appropriate steps have been taken by the Government of Iraq to safeguard against transferring or otherwise providing such assistance to violent extremist organizations." The bill would require the Administration to report on any such transfers and on end-use monitoring and assistance security arrangements in Iraq.

Iraqi Kurdish and Sunni Arab Forces

U.S. training and advisory programs in Iraq also include efforts to support Kurdish *peshmerga* and Sunni Arab tribal forces affiliated with Iraq's national government. Current U.S. policy provides U.S. material and advisory support to these forces in coordination with the national government in Baghdad. This policy corresponds with the Iraqi's government's request and reflects U.S. law that identifies countries and international organizations as the specified lawful recipients of direct U.S. security assistance.

To date, Congress has adopted Iraq-specific legislation authorizing U.S. assistance to Kurdish, Sunni Arab, and other security forces provided that these forces are affiliated with the Iraqi government. The FY2015 NDAA (Section 1236 of P.L. 113-291) authorized the provision of assistance to security forces "of or associated with the Government of Iraq," as well as "tribal security forces or other local security forces, with a national security mission." For the specific training of the 12 brigades discussed above.[50] Several legislative proposals in the 114th Congress would authorize the direct provision of U.S. assistance to Kurdish and/or other non-national level security forces in Iraq, more broadly subject to several conditions. These proposals have been the subject of considerable debate in Iraq (see "Defining the Way Forward in Iraq" and "FY2016 Budget Requests for Foreign Operations and Defense" below).

Support for Kurdish Forces

The central government in Baghdad and the KRG have had deep differences over territory, the exportation of oil, Kurdish ambitions for independence, and other issues. However, the threat posed by the Islamic State has led the two to make common cause, and since the crisis began, Baghdad has permitted the United States to transfer some of the ISF's weapons to the *peshmerga*.[51] As noted above, current U.S. policy plans for the training and equipping of three Kurdish *peshmerga* brigades as a component of the broader effort to develop the ISF. A "Building Partnership Capacity" training site has been established near Erbil where Kurdish forces are receiving U.S. training. A joint operation center established in Erbil also serves the headquarters for the U.S. advisory mission for *peshmerga* forces. A number of European countries, such as the United Kingdom, Germany, and France, also have been supplying weaponry to the *peshmerga*.

Baghdad reportedly also agreed to facilitate the transfer of some U.S. weapons to the *peshmerga,* although Kurdish officials have since expressed complaints about the willingness of Baghdad-authorities to approve weapons transfers.[52] KRG forces received 25 of the 250 MRAP vehicles supplied to Iraq in December 2014 and January 2015, and have received 1,000 anti-tank missiles.[53] During his May 2015 visit to Washington, DC, KRG President Masoud Barzani stated he had received "assurances" from Administration officials that further U.S. weapons deliveries to the *peshmerga* would occur.[54]

Congress has taken direct interest in the role of the *peshmerga* in efforts to combat the Islamic State organization and continues to conduct oversight on the delivery of U.S. assistance and training to Kurdish forces. The FY2015 NDAA joint explanatory statement prepared by House and Senate defense committee leaders states:

> We note the significant contribution that Kurdish security forces have made to countering ISIL's advance. We understand that the administration's plan includes assistance to train and equip 3 brigades of Kurdish *peshmerga*. Accordingly, we expect that a significant portion of the assistance under this authority will be provided to meet the requirements of the Kurdish security forces and urge the Secretary of Defense to ensure that such assistance is delivered in a timely manner to such forces. We further expect the Secretary of Defense to keep the congressional defense committees fully informed as this plan is developed and implemented, including any arrangements to ensure that such assistance for Kurdish security forces is promptly delivered to those forces.

State Department appropriations for FY2015 assistance to Iraq also are eligible for assistance to the Kurdistan Regional Government (Section 7041(c) of Division J, P.L. 113-235).

Support for Arab Sunni Forces

U.S. training and engagement with Arab Sunni tribal forces at Al Asad air base in western Iraq continues, with members of the Jughayf, Albu Mahal, and Albu Nimr tribes participating.[55] The reconstitution of the Anbar provincial police and recruitment to the Anbar-based 7th Iraqi Army division also are planned, as noted above.

In early May 2015, Iraqi authorities launched new training efforts for some Sunni tribal fighters from Anbar Province under the auspices of the government-affiliated Popular Mobilization Force program in eastern Anbar Province.[56] According to press accounts, the Iraqi Defense Ministry planned to oversee training for the forces, which was intended to produce a force of 6,000-8,000 vetted personnel. The fighters were to be armed in part with Iraqi Soviet-bloc weaponry set to be freed up by the provision of newer U.S. weapons to Iraqi Security Forces.[57] U.S. officials have expressed confidence that this initiative will be expedited given the subsequent fall of Ramadi to Islamic State forces and report that weapons delivery arrangements have now been clarified.[58]

The Popular Mobilization training began and Ramadi fell as Iraqi leaders remained divided over other proposals to create forces to fight the Islamic State in Anbar Province. Some Anbar Sunnis reject the entry of some Shiite-dominated Popular Mobilization Force units and would prefer that a locally led and staffed security force fight alongside the ISF in the province. Iraq's cabinet has approved draft legislation to authorize the creation of provincially aligned National Guard forces, and the Council of Representatives (COR) continues to debate the matter, with supporters calling for the prompt passage of the law and opponents warning that the creation of provincially aligned or commanded forces could facilitate the sectarian break-up of Iraq. The COR has worked on completing its second reading of the law after Ramadi's fall, with some dispute over committee consideration of the bill and its terms. Some Sunni politicians reportedly had slowed consideration of the bill in an attempt to extract greater concessions from other Baghdad leaders to ensure provincial level rather than national level command of national guard forces.[59] Some Shiite politicians reportedly seek to make the Popular Mobilization Forces the basis for the national guard and support the expansion of Sunni recruitment to the PMF under national government command.

Ongoing U.S. debate about proposals in the 114th Congress to directly arm certain security forces in Iraq (including Sunni tribal or "national guard" forces) appear to be influencing parallel debates in the COR concerning the draft national guard legislation, with uncertain prospects (see "Defining the Way Forward in Iraq" and "FY2016 Budget Requests for Foreign Operations and Defense" below).[60]

U.S. Training and Equipment for Vetted Syrians[61]

Several hundred U.S. military training personnel and a similar number of support personnel have deployed in support of a program authorized by Congress in 2014 to train and equip vetted Syrians to fight the Islamic State and promote a negotiated solution to Syria's civil war. According to Administration officials, the program intends to field a force of 5,400 vetted Syrians a year for each of three-years. Congress authorized such training and assistance in the FY2015 NDAA (H.R. 3979, P.L. 113-291) and FY2015 appropriations act (H.R. 83, P.L. 113-235). Initial funding for the program was approved by congressional defense committees in December 2014 under authority originally provided by Congress in the FY2015 continuing appropriations resolution of September 2014 (H.J.Res. 124, P.L. 113-164).

In early 2015, U.S. officials began engaging with different Syrian groups in order to identify potential recruits for the program and working with partner governments for assistance in vetting participants. Press reports citing unnamed U.S. officials suggested that fighting in Syria and uncertainties among Syrian opposition members and their regional backers about the program's purpose and about the general level of U.S. support for anti-Asad efforts delayed the program to some extent.[62]

Nevertheless, as of late March, U.S. officials reportedly had identified more than 2,000 planned participants and vetted 400 of them. Training began for the first batch of 90 recruits in early May.[63] U.S. officials have declined to publicly identify locations where training will take place, but various press reports claim that Turkey, Jordan, Saudi Arabia, and Qatar have agreed to host program activities. In late March, the United Kingdom announced it would support the U.S. training program by sending 75 training personnel to participate.

The Administration's FY2016 Defense appropriations request seeks $600 million in additional U.S. funding for the program with the goal of training a further 5400 personnel to add to the roughly 3000 planned to be trained using FY2015 funding. House and Senate versions of the FY2016 defense appropriations acts under consideration as of June 2015 (H.R. 2685) would appropriate that amount. The House and Senate versions of the FY2016 National Defense Authorization Act (H.R. 1735 and S. 1376) would authorize the appropriation of funding for the program, and would create new reporting and certification requirements relative to the provision of U.S. support to U.S.-trained fighters in the event of their attack by pro-Asad or Islamic State forces (see "Syria-Related Provisions" below).

Some Syrian opposition members and their U.S. supporters have criticized the Administration's training plans as insufficient in size and speed. Others disagree strategically with President Obama and argue that U.S.-backed forces should be trained for offensive operations against the Syrian government. U.S. defense officials said in early March and in early May that the Obama Administration was still considering what levels and types of support and defense assistance to supply to the trained personnel if they come under attack by pro-Asad forces.[64] House and Senate versions of FY2016 defense authorization legislation would require Administration reporting on the requirements for and provision of such support. For further discussion of these critiques and policy options under consideration, see "Defining the Way Forward in Syria" below.

Disrupting IS Financing[65]

The United States is pursuing a policy to reduce the financial resources available to the Islamic State focuses on disrupting IS revenue streams, limiting the group's access to formal financial systems, and imposing sanctions on the group's senior leadership and financial facilitators.[66]

Disrupting revenue streams. Under Secretary of the Treasury for Terrorism and Financial Intelligence David Cohen stated in late 2014 that the United States seeks to disrupt the group's revenue streams by targeting those who refine, transport, handle, or sell IS oil. The United States is also working with regional partners to identify cross-border smuggling routes and persons involved in smuggling networks. The United States has urged United Nations (U.N.) member states to help cut off resources to the Islamic State, and the U.N. Security Council in September passed resolution 2178 and 2199 to combat the flow of money and foreign fighters to the Islamic State and the Al Qaeda-affiliated *Jabhat al Nusra* (Support Front). However, observers have stated that while some countries in the region have passed legislation aimed at curbing the flow of funds to terrorist groups, these laws are often not implemented or enforced. Moreover, foreign donations comprise only a small portion of the Islamic State's income.[67] A U.S. military operation in Syria in May 2015 killed a senior Islamic State official reportedly involved in oil-related transactions for the group.

In addition to financial and political measures, the United States is also employing military means to target IS funding streams. Beginning in August 2014, U.S. military strikes against the Islamic State have targeted oil facilities, including collection points and mobile refineries. In a November hearing, Cohen reported that the Islamic State's revenue from oil sales had dropped from $1 million a day to several million dollars a week.[68] In January, U.S. Secretary of State John Kerry stated that coalition strikes had destroyed nearly 200 oil and gas facilities used by the Islamic State.[69] The resulting loss of revenue, Kerry stated, was restricting the group's operations and in some cases limiting its ability to pay salaries.

Restricting access to the financial system. Cohen noted that the United States aims to restrict the Islamic State's access to the international financial system and to limit its ability to move, store, and use funds it acquires locally. In particular, the United States works with Iraqi authorities, banks' headquarters, and the international financial community to prevent the Islamic State from using local bank branches in areas under its control. However, Iraqi sources in January stated that the Islamic State had established its own bank in Mosul, which granted loans and accepted deposits.[70]

Financial sanctions. The United States also has imposed sanctions against IS officials and their external financial backers. On September 24, the Department of the Treasury designated 12 individuals for their role in soliciting funds, procuring military equipment, and recruiting foreign fighters, two of whom are based in Syria and are associated with the Islamic State.[71] To date, few members of the Islamic State have been designated by the Department of the Treasury; U.S. officials have said this is in part due to the challenges in identifying individuals with a foothold in the formal financial system.[72]

U.N. Security Council Resolution 2199 (February 2015) condemns engagement in direct or indirect trade, particularly in oil and oil products, "with ISIL, ANF, and any other individuals, groups, undertakings and entities designated as associated with Al Qaeda." The resolution reaffirms several requirements to restrict flows of arms, combat financing, and prevent trade in Syrian and Iraqi cultural property. The resolution also establishes a reporting mechanism on international implementation of existing related resolutions.

Restricting Flows of Foreign Fighters

U.S. officials from the intelligence community, State Department, and other agencies concerned with domestic security continue to assess, monitor, and respond to threats posed by foreign fighters in Iraq and Syria. Diplomatic and intelligence efforts focus on coordinating with source, transit, and returnee destination countries to strengthen shared responses and preventive measures.[73] In March 2014, the State Department named Ambassador Robert Bradtke as "senior adviser for partner engagement on Syria foreign fighters," and former U.S. Ambassador to Bahrain Thomas Krajeski replaced Bradtke in that role in January 2015.

Although the Islamic State organization is considered a direct threat to U.S. interests in the Middle East, it is unclear whether it currently poses direct threats to U.S. homeland security. A shooting attack by U.S. nationals in Texas in May 2015 was claimed by IS personnel overseas, but U.S. officials had not suggested any direct operational links between the attackers and the Islamic State organization as of May 11. The Texas attack followed a spate of similar attacks in Europe and elsewhere, in which the alleged perpetrators appeared to be inspired by the Islamic State but not necessarily operationally linked to it. In November 2014, National Counterterrorism Center (NCTC) Director Nicholas Rasmussen said in congressional testimony that "the [ISIL] threat beyond the Middle East is real, although thus far limited in sophistication. However, if left unchecked, over time we can expect ISIL's capabilities to mature, and the threat to the United States homeland ultimately to increase."[74]

More recently, Rasmussen estimated that more than 20,000 foreign fighters from as many as 90 countries, including more than 3,400 Westerners, may have travelled to Syria since 2011 in a trend that U.S. officials have described as "unprecedented."[75] According to U.S. officials, approximately 180 U.S. citizens have traveled or attempted to travel to Syria to support armed groups there since the start of the Syrian conflict in 2011, and approximately 12 Americans were believed by U.S. officials to have been fighting there as of September 2014. As noted above, anti-IS operations have killed thousands of IS personnel since August 2014, including an unknown number of foreign fighters. In May 2015, an unnamed senior State Department official said:[76]

> ...we've never seen something like this. We've never seen a terrorist organization with 22,000 foreign fighters from a hundred countries all around the world. To put it in context – again, the numbers are fuzzy – but it's about double of what went into Afghanistan over 10 years in the war against the Soviet Union. Those jihadi fighters were from a handful of countries. These guys are coming from a hundred different countries. You combine that with social media, their efforts to inspire homegrown attacks, not even to have fighters come and train but do attacks at home, this is a formidable, enormous threat.

The U.S. government has supported the adoption of several U.N. Security Council Resolutions to strengthen international sanctions and halt flows of foreign fighters and financing to the Islamic State, Jabhat al Nusra, and Al Qaeda-affiliated entities. Resolution 2170 (August 2014) calls upon all Member States "to take national measures to suppress the flow of foreign terrorist fighters to, and bring to justice, in accordance with applicable international law, foreign terrorist fighters of, ISIL, ANF and all other individuals, groups, undertakings and entities associated with Al Qaida," and reiterates Member States' obligation to prevent terrorist travel, limit supplies of weapons and financing, and exchange information on the groups.

Resolution 2178 (September 2014) requires Member States, consistent with international law, to prevent the "recruiting, organizing, transporting or equipping of individuals who travel to a State other than their States of residence or nationality for the purpose of the perpetration, planning of, or participation in terrorist acts.” In December 2014, Ambassador Bradkte said, “Several countries have already enacted or proposed legislation to permit [prosecution for foreign fighter facilitation]; other countries have stepped up their enforcement of existing laws. We continue to urge partners to meet their obligations under UNSCR 2178, and are offering assistance to partners who may need help in doing so.”[77]

Achievements and Views on Effectiveness

Experts and officials are debating the effectiveness of U.S. strategy overall, and its individual elements. Administration officials have identified areas where they claim progress has been made in implementing U.S. strategy to date,[78] but have stated clearly that it may take months, and in some cases years, to achieve the full range of U.S. objectives. In congressional testimony and public statements early in 2015, U.S. civilian and military leaders described the Islamic State organization as having assumed a defensive posture in Iraq and Syria in response to counteroffensives by coalition and local forces. On March 3, General Austin described the group as “losing this fight” and reported that anti-IS operations had killed more than 8,500 fighters, destroyed hundreds of vehicles and heavy weapons systems, and significantly degraded IS command and control capabilities.[79] In April 2015, President Obama said, “About a quarter of the territory fallen under Daesh control has been recovered. Thousands of strikes have not only taken ISIL fighters off the war theater, but their infrastructure has been deteriorated and decayed.”[80]

However, noting that IS forces continue to show offensive capability in Iraq and Syria, Administration officials have more recently qualified the degree of success achieved to date and reminded the public that U.S. plans and strategy envision a multi-year effort that is likely to suffer setbacks. Administration officials and military officers have described the fall of Ramadi as one such setback, rather than accepting the arguments made by some that the loss of the city is a harbinger of strategic defeat. U.S. officials continue to suggest that the biggest threat to sustainable success in the anti-IS campaign may be the potential for renewed intensification of sectarian tension in Iraq or the persistence of leadership weakness in the Iraqi military.

Administration critics argue that U.S. strategy lacks effective partners who can advance against Islamic State-held territory on the ground and suffers from a basic contradiction in not confronting the regime of President Asad of Syria. These critics assert that achieving stated Administration objectives requires U.S. or other ground combat troops and expansion of the mission to include compelling Asad to accept a political solution that will allow more pressure to be brought to bear against the Islamic State in its Syrian strongholds.

POLICY DEBATES AND RELATED LEGISLATIVE ISSUES

Congressional Consideration of and Concerns about the President's IS AUMF Proposal[81]

The President has stated that the Authorization for Use of Military Force ("2001 AUMF"; P.L. 107-40) and the Authorization for Use of Military Force Against Iraq Resolution of 2002 ("2002 AUMF"; P.L. 107-243) provide authorization for the current U.S. military campaign against the Islamic State in Iraq and Syria, as well as the Khorasan Group of Al Qaeda in Syria. On February 11, 2015, however, the President provided Congress with a draft proposal for a new AUMF targeting the Islamic State (IS AUMF),[82] stating in an accompanying letter that he "can think of no better way for the Congress to join [the President] in supporting our Nation's security than by enacting this legislation, which would show the world we are united in our resolve to counter the threat posed by ISIL."[83] The President's proposal would authorize the use of U.S. Armed Forces that he deems "necessary and appropriate" against the Islamic State and associated persons or forces. In the proposed authorization, "the term 'associated persons or forces' means individuals and organizations fighting for, on behalf of, or alongside ISIL or any closely related successor entity in hostilities against the United States or its coalition partners." The authorization does not include authority for the use of U.S. Armed Forces for "enduring offensive ground combat operations." The proposal's authorization would terminate three years after enactment, and contains a provision repealing the 2002 AUMF upon enactment. The President would be required to report to Congress at least every six months on actions taken under the proposed IS AUMF.

Since the President proposed this new IS AUMF, several Members of Congress have expressed various concerns over its provisions, and Obama Administration officials have made a number of statements in response to the issues raised. The Senate Foreign Relations and House Foreign Affairs

Committees, as well as both houses' Armed Services Committees, have held several hearings during which issues concerning the proposal have been discussed, including the following:

- With regard to the proposed IS AUMF's prohibition on "enduring offensive ground combat operations," there have been questions about what this phrase effectively prohibits. Administration officials have stated that the phrase is not based in military terminology, but instead reflects presidential intent. The President's letter states that it is designed to allow limited ground operations, such as rescuing U.S. personnel, enabling kinetic strikes, gathering and sharing intelligence, and providing advice and assistance to partner forces. Other Administration officials have stated that the prohibition is intended to prohibit lengthy, large-scale ground combat operations such as those undertaken in Iraq from 2003 to 2011, or in Afghanistan since 2001, but that it would not prohibit the current use of ground forces and would be flexible enough to allow other, possibly expanded uses of ground forces in the future. Some Members of Congress have stated that this interpretation of the prohibition might be too broad, as it could lead to sizable and lengthy ground combat operations against the Islamic State and other groups.
- The President's proposal does not include any geographical limitation, and specifically authorizes military force against "associated persons or forces," possibly enabling the use of military force in countries other than Iraq and Syria. In recent months, elements of the Islamic State have carried out attacks in countries other than Iraq and Syria, and new groups in still more countries have pledged allegiance and cooperation with the Islamic State, potentially greatly expanding the geographic reach of the proposed IS AUMF. Some argue that any AUMF should have a geographic restriction, because although the target may be a non-state actor, Congress should enact a specific authorization to allow U.S. armed Forces to use military force in each country where that non-state actor operates. Specific concern has been expressed over the association of the Boko Haram group in Nigeria with the Islamic State, as it highlights the possibly global nature of the proposed IS AUMF's authority. Obama Administration officials do not seem to agree with this approach, stating that the United States must be able to strike IS and associated forces wherever they operate, and to deny "safe haven" to such forces.

- Although the President states in his letter that he still intends to engage Congress in reforming the 2001 AUMF, his proposal does not contain a provision that repeals or sunsets that measure, unlike most of the IS AUMF proposals previously introduced. Administration officials have accepted the concept of a three-year sunset for the authority contained in the proposed IS AUMF, as it would ensure that Congress and a new President would have the opportunity to revisit the authorization. Some Members have asked why the same principle does not apply to revisiting the 2001 AUMF, which the executive still relies on to combat Al Qaeda, the Taliban, and various other terror groups in several countries. In addition, because the President and several Administration officials have repeatedly asserted that the 2001 AUMF already provides sufficient authority to conduct the military campaign against the Islamic State, some Members question whether any restrictions on the duration of a new IS AUMF will have real effect if the President can simply rely on 2001 AUMF authority after the IS AUMF expires.
- There have been questions as to whether the proposed IS AUMF provides any authority to use military force against forces of the Syrian government either offensively or defensively to protect anti-Asad forces in Syria being trained and equipped by the United States. Administration officials have stated that the IS AUMF proposal relates only to combatting the Islamic State and associated forces, and does not authorize the President to order the use of force against Syrian government forces, including to defend vetted Syrian rebel groups. The possibility that the United States would want to extend authorities to protect such rebel groups might be discussed separately, Administration officials have stated, as it could be important to the morale of such groups and the success of U.S. policy in Syria.

Defining the Way Forward in Iraq

Efforts to reconquer areas of Iraq held by the Islamic State organization pose several dilemmas for Iraqi leaders and communities. On one hand, the threat posed by the IS advance in 2014 served as a unifying force in Iraqi political and security debates, bringing together leaders and forces with differing priorities in support of the general objective of resisting IS forces. On the other hand, the need to respond to the IS threat hardened differences of opinion concerning the future of Iraq's security forces and underlying political relationships between the national government and various sub-national groups. Some Iraqis argue that a strong central government directing the operations of national security forces with unified command, control, and logistics capabilities is the only prescription for evicting IS fighters. Other Iraqis argue that a decentralized political arrangement backed by nationally recognized and empowered, but regionally organized security forces will be best able to durably defeat the Islamic State.

At the heart of these differences of opinion are unresolved ethnic, sectarian, political, and personal disputes; legacies of mutual distrust among some Iraqi Kurds, Sunnis and Shiite Arabs, and minority groups; and suspicions of foreign intentions toward Iraq. Some members of different Iraqi factions appear skeptical of each other's motives and express concern that outsiders, including the United States, seek to use the current security crisis as a means of dividing Iraq into smaller ethnic, sectarian, and regional entities for their own purposes.

Statements by some U.S. and Iraqi leaders appear to reflect an understanding of these challenges and a desire to overcome them. U.S. policy seeks to support the security of a unified Iraq through the development of the ISF and other forces affiliated with Iraq's national government. Prime Minister Abadi actively engages with key leaders in different parts of Iraq in support of his government's own plans to defeat IS forces through a mixture of ISF operations, regionally organized security force operations, and coalition assistance. He continues to praise the support offered by coalition partners, while insisting that such support continue to be channeled through and/or delivered in coordination with the national government in Baghdad.

Some Iraqi and U.S. critics charge that the performance of the Iraqi government in the fight against the Islamic State to date has been lacking and contend that Baghdad has failed to direct necessary assistance to Kurdish and Sunni forces or to adequately constrain some Iran-backed Shiite militia forces engaged in the anti-IS fight. Some legislative proposals in the 114th Congress reflect these views and provide authorization for direct U.S. assistance to specific forces in Iraq in addition to ongoing engagement with the ISF. Iraqis who are skeptical of U.S. intentions or who express concern about the devolution of security authority to sectarian and regional entities have in turn rejected proposals that take the direct assistance approach.

Iraqi Prime Minister Haider al Abadi has clearly expressed his fears that Iraq may become a battlefield in a struggle among its neighbors and other foreign powers to shape the future of Iraq's constituent communities. He also has identified challenges associated with the Iraqi military's limitations and its consequent reliance on irregular forces aligned with ethnic, sectarian, or regional identity groups. On April 3, he told the German media outlet Spiegel that,

> There are a lot of dangers that we are not seeing yet, and for which the seeds are now planted. No. 1: When we succeed in driving the terrorists out of the cities and towns, it is most likely they will still have hotspots in Iraq. They will try to agitate the population again. No. 2: We have many thousands of civilians who rose to defend their own country against this terrorist threat. They have arms at their disposal, and they are very powerful because they are ideologically motivated. Honestly, it would be a challenge to deal with this.[84]

Abadi's appeals for support for the Iraqi military, including expedited or expanded shipments of arms, and his insistence that support from the United States and others be channeled through Baghdad and his chain of command may be closely related to these concerns and others regarding the future of the KRG and the *peshmerga* and the future of Sunni Arab forces. Abadi's Iraqi and U.S. critics hold him partially responsible for perpetuating political and security arrangements that have prolonged Sunni and Kurdish fears of domination by the Baghdad government and that have preserved a role for Iran-backed Shiite militias in the fight against the Islamic State.

From the U.S. perspective, the relative role and behavior of Iraq's regular and irregular forces and the mechanisms used for the delivery of U.S. assistance to different Iraqi entities appear directly related to the desired end state for Iraq. U.S. officials continue to emphasize the importance of nonsectarian behavior in their engagement with Iraqi leaders and military commanders, and U.S. officials have reiterated their support for the unity of Iraq during recent visits by Iraqi leaders to Washington.[85] There are some indications that the U.S. military has calibrated its assistance during some anti-IS operations to reinforce this message, such as when U.S. airstrikes on Tikrit reportedly were predicated on the withdrawal of Iranian advisors from the area. On March 30, U.S. Secretary of Defense Ashton Carter said,

> the critical feature to us is that the operation on the ground be under the command and control of the government of Iraq, and that's important because our whole strategy is to enable a multi-sectarian government of Iraq to make sure that when ISIL is defeated in Iraq, that it stays defeated. ... one of the things that we were wanting to ensure before we conducted airstrikes in the area of Tikrit, and we understand that the forces that are around the city of

> Tikrit are of several different types, but the ones that we are supporting are those that are in the command and control of the government of Iraq.[86]

In subsequent weeks, including in the aftermath of Ramadi's fall to the Islamic State, U.S. officials have reiterated their willingness to support Iraqi Security Forces and other anti-IS forces in Iraq provided that they are under the command and control of the central government in Baghdad or in the case of the KRG and *peshmerga*, operating in line with Iraq's constitution.

Even though the ISF and *peshmerga* have made some progress in their fight against the Islamic State in recent months, further successes are fraught with obstacles and difficulties. Efforts to reverse IS gains in Anbar Province and notional offensives against Islamic State strongholds in Mosul may require difficult Iraqi and coalition decisions about the terms for and scope of assistance to the ISF and security forces associated with the government. Despite some of the compromises made by Prime Minister Abadi with the Sunni community, many of Iraq's Sunnis still appear unwilling in the absence of further commitments or support to counter the Islamic State in the ways many took U.S.-aided action against the Islamic State's precursor—Al Qaeda in Iraq—in 2006 and 2007 (the so-called *sahwa*, or awakening). Kurdish leaders continue to cooperate with Baghdad but also seek the delivery of new heavier and longer-range weaponry— whether directly supplied or otherwise—in order to counter weaponry in the hands of IS forces in northern Iraq.[87]

Whether or not Prime Minister Abadi can win Sunni and Kurdish trust may depend largely on whether he and other top Shiite leaders in the central government demonstrate a willingness to accommodate local views; provide security assistance; credibly exercise control over Shiite militia groups; and/or fairly administer government resources. Nevertheless, providing weapons, training, and autonomy to the KRG, Sunni groups, or other sub-national entities could incur opposition from Iraqis who fear that more potent arsenals or increased political authority could enable sub-national groups to divide the country. Specific concerns also persist outside the KRG about Kurdish forces retaining control of the disputed territory of Kirkuk, which the *peshmerga* seized as the ISF collapsed in June 2014. These dynamics significantly complicate U.S. decisions about the provision of assistance and coordination with different Iraqi entities in the fight against the Islamic State.

Potential Strategy Changes?

Prior to the Islamic State capture of Ramadi, U.S. officials and outside experts had publicly speculated about next steps in the Iraq campaign, with the underlying assumption that existing strategy and resource levels would eventually defeat the Islamic State in Iraq. There had been a debate over whether Iraq and the coalition should focus on liberating Mosul, or instead on expelling the Islamic State from Anbar Province. The Islamic State capture of Ramadi has prompted speculation that, to accomplish the stated objective of defeating the Islamic State, U.S. strategy and resource levels might change. White House officials have signaled that they do not intend to change the overarching strategic approach, but President Obama has announced plans to deploy additional training personnel, and U.S. military leaders have acknowledged ongoing consideration of new policy recommendations and operational approaches to achieve current strategic goals.[88] The following are options being recommended by experts and some Members of Congress:

Deploy Ground Combat Units

Some recommend that the need to defeat the Islamic State is sufficiently critical to merit reintroduction of ground combat troops to Iraq.[89] President Obama has repeatedly ruled out the deployment of ground combat units, maintaining that U.S. troops will not fix the underlying political problems that facilitated or caused the IS-led insurrection.

Move U.S. Advisers and Airstrike Targeters Closer to Front Lines

Outgoing Chairman of the Joint Chiefs of Staff Martin Dempsey said in November 2014 that as the campaign requires more complex operations by Iraqi Security Forces, he might recommend that U.S. advisers accompany Iraqi forces.[90] A related recommendation some military experts make is to position U.S. military personnel closer to front lines as "forward air controllers" to be able to better target Islamic State forces. No decision on any of these options has been announced, but in February 2015, President Obama sent to Congress a request for a new Authorization for the Use of Military Force that in the Administration's view would, if approved, provide flexibility to undertake these options as well as conduct ground combat operations.[91]

Arm and Train Sunni Tribal Fighters

Some suggest that the key to defeating the Islamic State is to use many of the same Sunni tribal fighters that helped U.S. forces defeat Al Qaeda in Iraq during 2006-2011. Those who advocate this option assert that it is an extension of existing U.S. efforts to persuade Iraq's Shiite leadership to arm Sunni units under central government command and to undertake additional steps to win Sunni loyalties. Some Sunni Arab Iraqis are seeking a broader devolution of power from Baghdad in conjunction with these steps and specifically seek authority for Sunni aligned forces to operate under local rather than national command. As noted above (see "Support for Arab Sunni Forces"), U.S. personnel in Iraq have begun training some Sunni tribesmen, suggesting that this option is already being pursued, although perhaps not on the terms or to the extent that advocates of this option seek.

Support Shiite Militia Forces

Another option proposed by some Iraqi officials and outside experts would be to drop U.S. objections to supporting with airstrikes operations by Shiite militia and Popular Mobilization Units. Suggesting some Administration openness to forms of this option, U.S. Ambassador to Iraq Stuart Jones reportedly told some Iraqi Sunni figures that the United States would conduct airstrikes in support of forces that are under Iraq command, but not those under the command of Iranian advisers.[92] On May 26, State Department spokesman Jeff Rathke reiterated "we will continue to support all efforts by Iraqi forces under the command and control of the Iraqi Government."

Defining the Way Forward in Syria

President Obama said in September 2014 that U.S. engagement in Syria would remain focused "narrowly" on assisting Syrians in combatting the Islamic State, while continuing "to look for opportunities" to support a political resolution to Syria's conflict.[93] After a May 2015 visit to Moscow, U.S. Special Envoy for Syria Daniel Rubenstein said "the Syrian regime's brutal actions have contributed to the growth of extremism" and said defeating extremists in Syria "would require both military steps and a comprehensive political solution that addresses the legitimate grievances of the Syrian people."[94] Rubinstein also "stressed" that President Asad's "continued presence atop the Syrian regime is exacerbating sectarianism and extremism not only in Syria, but in the region."

Some Syrian political and military opposition forces appear to resent what they see as the United States' narrow focus on fighting Sunni extremists in Syria, and some have indicated that they may insist on broader support for their anti-Asad goals as a condition of working with the U.S.-backed coalition against the Islamic State. These parties also question why the United States and coalition partners are willing to act militarily to halt Islamic State atrocities but not to protect Syrian civilians from attacks by government forces or opposition groups.

In this context, U.S. strikes against Islamic State targets and other terrorist groups in Syria are illuminating several dilemmas faced by the Administration. On one hand, Syrian opposition forces who have been fighting the Islamic State welcome U.S. and coalition assistance in their campaign, but question why the United States does not take military action against the Asad government or take more robust action to degrade IS capabilities in Syria. The Administration's policy initiatives reflect its intention to pressure the Asad government into negotiating with opposition groups and fulfilling its pledges with regard to chemical weapons. At the same time, U.S. officials appear to be balancing these goals with concerns that a full scale degradation of Islamic State forces or of pro-Asad forces could have unintended consequences. Specifically, U.S. officials may be concerned that a more aggressive campaign against the Islamic State may take military pressure off the Asad regime or create opportunities for other extremist groups such as the Al Qaeda-affiliated Jabhat al Nusra to advance.

Some U.S. critics of the Obama Administration's approach to the conflict and terrorism threats in Syria argue that current U.S. strategy lacks effective Syrian partners willing or able to advance against Islamic State and/or Al Qaeda-affiliate-held territory on the ground. These critics suggest the United States should either abandon its efforts to support a vetted partner force in Syria or drastically expand the size and scope of those efforts to create a more formidable partner force. Others critics argue that U.S. strategy is built on faulty assumptions or priorities because it is not based on an inherently confrontational posture toward the Asad regime. These critics argue that Asad's departure or demise is the key to resolving the underlying conflict that has created opportunity for extremists to thrive. Whether or how Asad's departure would immediately change the fortunes of the Islamic State in Syria is uncertain. Still other critics assert that achieving stated Administration objectives will likely require U.S. or other ground combat troops or an expansion of the planned "train and equip" program for vetted Syrians to focus more aggressively on pressuring Asad to accept a negotiated solution.

Opponents of deeper U.S. engagement with or support for Syrian combatants have argued that the United States cannot guarantee that provided material assistance will not fall in to the hands of extremist groups or the Asad government. Others fear that by arming and training Syrian opposition members overtly or by supporting such forces in the field, the United States may be making itself a combatant in Syria's civil war. Still others argue that the wider international precedents set by U.S. assistance for or intervention on behalf of trained opposition members risk undermining broader U.S. support for principles of nonintervention and sovereignty or policy goals in specific conflicts.

For the moment, the Administration does not appear to be prioritizing the underlying conflict in Syria. Rather, it is taking steps in Syria designed to mitigate terrorism threats and advance U.S. goals for stabilizing Iraq. This approach could weaken the Islamic State to the extent that it forces the group to abandon strategic, lucrative territory that it controls in Iraq. Coalition strikes and U.S.-backed partner forces may also deprive the group of some important Iraq-based leaders and fighters and some of the powerful military equipment it has captured there. However, the "Iraq first" and "ISIL first" approach could so alienate potential Syrian partners that if the United States later decides to give priority to the stabilization of Syria it will find itself facing a more skeptical populace. Anti-IS actions in Syria also may create opportunities for other Syria-based Islamist groups and/or empower the Syrian government at the expense of other elements of the Syrian opposition.

At present, senior Administration officials have told Congress and the press that the Administration is actively considering whether or how to provide military protection to U.S.-trained Syrians participating in the train and equip program.[95] The prospect that Islamic State forces or pro-Asad forces may attack U.S.-trained Syrians exists, and it remains to be determined whether, how, under what circumstances, and on what authority the U.S. military may provide armed protection for trainees. As described below ("Syria-Related Provisions"), House and Senate versions of the FY2016 National Defense Authorization Act would require Administration reporting on this issue. In the case of potential attack by Syrian government forces, for example, such protection could entail attacks against Syrian military targets, with uncertain implications for the conflict in Syria and for anti-Islamic State operations in Iraq, where Asad's principal foreign support—Iran—is working to combat the Islamic State in parallel with the coalition.

Iranian Involvement in the Iraq and Syria Crises

Iran opposes the Islamic State's advance in Iraq and has been generally cooperating with U.S. policy there. However, the United States has ruled out formally bringing Iran into any U.S.-led anti-Islamic State coalition and remains concerned about Iranian desires for influence in Baghdad and Erbil and Iranian support for some Shiite militia forces. On Syria, the United States and Iran have generally been on opposite sides: the United States supports Asad's ouster in favor of a transition regime, whereas Iran is materially supporting Asad's efforts to remain in power. Iran apparently views expanded U.S. efforts to provide support and training to Syrian opposition groups as a threat to its interests.

On Iraq, U.S. diplomats acknowledge that they have discussed the Islamic State crisis at margins of recent talks on Iran's nuclear program. Iran abandoned its longtime ally Maliki[96] and helped compel him to yield power in favor of Abadi. The U.S. State Department has consistently refuted assertions that the bilateral discussion on Iraq could provide Iran additional leverage in the ongoing nuclear talks with the United States and its partner countries.[97] However, President Obama has acknowledged sending a letter in November 2014 to Iran's Supreme Leader Ali Khamene'i, the contents of which have not been released but which was said to focus on the potential for further cooperation against the Islamic State if the issue of Iran's nuclear program were resolved.[98]

In actions that appear to further U.S. objectives in Iraq, Iran reportedly has been delivering arms and ammunition to the ISF and the *peshmerga*. In July 2014, Iran returned to Iraq about a dozen of the 100+ Iraqi combat aircraft that were flown to Iran at the start of the 1991 war between Iraq and the U.S.-led coalition. Iranian pilots apparently also are flying the aircraft: in July 2014 Iran announced that one of its pilots had died in operations in Iraq.[99] Iran reportedly has provided weapons to Syrian Kurds fighting Islamic State forces in northern Syria.

Many observers remain skeptical that the United States can or should cooperate with Iran in either Iraq or Syria. Iran helped establish many of the Shiite militias that fought the United States during 2003-2011, and reportedly has sent Islamic Revolutionary Guard-Quds Force (IRGC-QF) personnel into Iraq to advise some of the Shiite militias fighting alongside the ISF. On Syria, Iran continues to support Asad militarily, thereby countering U.S. efforts to compel Asad to yield power to a transition regime.

FY2016 Budget Requests for Foreign Operations and Defense

On February 2, 2015, the Obama Administration released its preliminary FY2016 budget requests for foreign operations and defense. The Administration is seeking funding to continue the current lines of effort in response to the Islamic State threat, as well as to respond to the challenges posed by the broader conflicts and regional displacements related to Syria and Iraq.

Select specific requests include

- **Iraq and Syria Train and Equip Programs**—The Department of Defense is requesting $715 million and $600 million for train and equip programs for Iraqis and Syrians respectively. These requests would fund continuation of programs initiated under authorities and funds first provided in FY2015 Defense authorization and appropriations bills. The monies would be drawn from FY2016 Department of the Army Operations and Maintenance Overseas Contingency Operations (O&M-OCO) funding. The Administration also seeks $250 million in Foreign Military Financing for Iraq.
- **Continued Support to Syrian Opposition Groups**—The State Department is requesting $65 million in Peacekeeping Operations-OCO (PKO-OCO) funding to provide nonlethal support to vetted, moderate armed opposition groups "to bolster their capacity, cohesion, and credibility" and "to strengthen linkages between armed and civilian actors." The Administration also is requesting $160 million in Economic Support Fund-OCO (ESF-OCO) funding to provide nonlethal assistance to other opposition groups and $10 million in International Narcotics Control and Law Enforcement (INCLE-OCO) funding for justice sector support in opposition-held areas.
- **Iraq and Syria-Related Humanitarian Funding**—The Administration is requesting $1.629 billion in Migration and Refugee Assistance-OCO (MRAOCO) and International Disaster Assistance-OCO (IDA-OCO) funding to support continuing U.S. contributions to humanitarian relief and host-country support programs related to Syrian and Iraqi refugees and internally displaced persons.
- **Counterterrorism Partnerships Fund (CTPF)**—The Administration requests FY2016 CTPF funds to address terrorist safe havens, including in Iraq and Syria; to mitigate foreign fighter flows;

and to counter Iranian support for terrorism, including its support for militia forces in Lebanon and Iraq.

Table 1. Select Iraq/Syria Related FY2016 Budget Requests for Foreign Operations and Defense
($ in millions)

Program/Account	Iraq	Syria	Jordan	Regional	Totals
Train and Equip Programs (DoD)	715	600			1315
INCLE-OCO	11	10			21
PKO-OCO		65			65
FMF-OCO	250		50		300
ESF-OCO	50	160	277.4		487.4
MRA-OCO				819	819
IDA-OCO				810	810
Totals	1026	835	327.4	1629	3817.4
Counterterrorism Partnerships Fund (CTPF)					
CTPF-State				390	
CTPF-DoD				2100	2490

Sources: FY2016 Congressional Budget Justifications for Defense Operations and Maintenance Funds and State Department Foreign Operations, February 2015.

Related Legislation in the 114th Congress

Syria-Related Provisions

The House-enrolled version of the FY2016 National Defense Authorization Act (Section 1225 of H.R. 1735) would authorize the appropriation of the President's requested $600 million for the Syria train and equip program in a stand-alone account. It would extend provisions in the existing authority that require the executive branch to submit reprogramming requests to congressional Defense committees when seeking to obligate funds appropriated to the account. The House version also would require the Administration to update and integrate its strategy reports to Congress on the campaigns in Syria and Iraq and certify that required forces have been established and deployed in support of the strategy and that required support will be provided to trained Syrians "consistent with the purposes" Congress has identified for the program. These purposes, as specified in the FY2015 legislation that established the program, are:

1) Defending the Syrian people from attacks by the Islamic State of Iraq and the Levant (ISIL), and securing territory controlled by the Syrian opposition.
2) Protecting the United States, its friends and allies, and the Syrian people from the threats posed by terrorists in Syria.
3) Promoting the conditions for a negotiated settlement to end the conflict in Syria.

The Senate Armed Services Committee-reported version of the FY2016 NDAA (Section 1208 of S. 1376) also would authorize the requested appropriation for the program and would require the Administration to provide “a detailed description of the military support the Secretary [of Defense] considers necessary to provide to recipients of assistance” in the Syria train and equip program “upon their return to Syria to make use of such assistance.” According to the bill, this support may include “1) Logistical support; (2) Defensive supportive fire; (3) Intelligence; (4) Medical support; (5) Any other support the Secretary considers appropriate for purposes of the report.” The bill stated that the report requirement should not be considered an authorization for the use of U.S. military force in Syria and states the report should include cost estimates and a description of steps taken to ensure that U.S. assistance does not benefit extremist groups or the Asad government.

On June 10, the House rejected an amendment offered to the FY2016 defense appropriations act (H.R. 2685) that would have stripped FY2016 funding for the Syria train and equip program (Roll no. 343 on H.R. 2685).

Iraq-Related Provisions

Reflecting President Obama’s request, the House-enrolled version of the FY2016 National Defense Authorization Act (H.R. 1735) would authorize the appropriation of $715 million in Overseas Contingency Operations (OCO) funding for security assistance to Iraqi security forces, including the Kurdish *peshmerga*; Sunni tribal security forces with a national security mission; and the proposed “Iraqi Sunni National Guard.” Other legislation introduced in the House (H.R. 1654) and Senate (S. 1188) also would authorize the conditional provision of U.S. assistance directly to Kurdish *peshmerga* forces. These bills would suggest, but would not require the U.S. government to consult with the

Baghdad government on authorized transfers or to notify Baghdad prior to authorized transfers.

On June 10, the House rejected an amendment offered to the FY2016 defense appropriations act that would have stripped FY2016 funding for the Iraq train and equip program (Roll no. 342 on H.R. 2685).

The Senate Armed Services Committee's reported version of the FY2016 NDAA (S. 1376) does not include new authorities or directions concerning the provision of direct assistance to individual forces in Iraq. Section 1229 of the SASC-reported version would express the sense of the Senate that the U.S. government should provide

> in an expeditious and responsive manner and without undue delay, the security forces of the Kurdistan Regional Government associated with the Government of Iraq with... anti-tank and anti-armor weapons, armored vehicles, long-range artillery, crew-served weapons and ammunition, secure command and communications equipment, body armor, helmets, logistics equipment, night optical devices, and other excess defense articles and military assistance considered appropriate by the President.

At present, virtually all U.S. assistance to security forces in Iraq, including Kurdish and Sunni tribal forces, is coordinated with and/or channeled through the Baghdad government.[100] This process reflects U.S. policy goals of promoting Iraq's unity under a non-sectarian national government, as discussed above (see "Train and Equip" Assistance" and "Defining the Way Forward in Iraq"). However, the process more generally reflects long-standing U.S. law and policy identifying countries (i.e. national governments) and international organizations as the specified lawful recipients of U.S. security assistance. Relevant provisions of the Arms Export Control Act (22 U.S.C. §2751 et seq.) and the Foreign Assistance Act of 1961 (22 U.S.C. §2151 et seq.) identify authorized recipients of U.S. defense and security assistance as a "country or international organization."[101] Because of this existing language in U.S. law, some of the legislative proposals cited above would, under certain circumstances and on certain terms, recognize specific Iraqi groups as the equivalent of "countries" relative to standing U.S. laws governing foreign security assistance. The original House Armed Services Committee-reported version of the FY2016 NDAA would have explicitly directed the executive branch to consider individual Iraqi forces as the equivalents of countries, which sparked considerable debate in Iraq (see below). The direct reference to countries was removed by a managers' amendment during floor consideration of the bill.

Supporters of the Iraq-related provisions in the House-enrolled version of the FY2016 NDAA and other proposals to allow direct support to the KRG argue that U.S. assistance should be leveraged to ensure that all elements of Iraqi society can defend themselves and are engaged in the fight against the Islamic State organization on a non-sectarian basis. Supporters further argue that legislative constructions in the proposals identify as eligible for such direct assistance only specific groups whose legitimacy is already recognized in Iraq's constitution and national laws (or may soon be in the case of national guard forces). Supporters of stand-alone KRG-specific legislation further argue that proposed assistance authorities would be temporary and would state that the President "should" consult with the Iraqi government and "should" notify Baghdad prior to authorized transfers.

One U.S. observer called the provision an "incredibly drastic change of U.S. policy in Iraq."[102] Iraqi critics of the proposals—mostly leaders and factions that dominate the government and security structure—argue that proposed provisions would undermine Iraqi sovereignty by allowing a foreign power to bypass the national government and could contribute to the de facto partitioning of the country through the strengthening of security forces aligned with sectarian and ethnic groups. U.S. legislative references to specific security forces and groups as the legal equivalents of countries appear to implicate broader concerns among some Iraqis about the security and political unity of their country. Whether or not forces named in the proposals such as the national guard will be under Iraqi national government command or provincial government command remains a matter of debate in Iraq's parliament.

On April 29, Iraqi Prime Minister Abadi issued a statement rejecting the terms of the House Armed Services Committee-reported version of the NDAA, saying it would increase divisiveness in Iraq and calling for it to be permanently withdrawn.[103] Iraq's Ministry of Foreign Affairs stated its "extreme rejection" of the bill and said "it harms Iraq's sovereignty and targets the Iraqi people's unity."[104] The Sunni and Kurdish members of the Council of Representatives (COR) reportedly walked out of a session of parliament that met to discuss the proposed shift in U.S. policy, with remaining Shiite members rejecting direct U.S. assistance to Iraqis other than via national government channels.[105]

Shiite religious figure and militia leader Muqtada al Sadr said the type of assistance the bill would authorize would be "the beginning of the division of Iraq" and he threatened to strike U.S. interests in Iraq and abroad if the bill's terms became U.S. policy.[106] The Imam Ali Brigades, a Shiite militia participating in the Popular Mobilization initiative, said "the American Congress's passing of a bill recognizing Sunnis and Kurds as separate states is a blatant interference... We will not allow you and your allies to partition Iraq."[107] Sadr and other Shiite figures have spoken out against alleged plots to divide Iraq in the past, but some Shiite militia forces reportedly accept direct security assistance from Iran and may make selective arguments against perceived outside interference to advance more narrow interests.

The Obama Administration has reiterated its view that U.S. assistance to Iraq should be coordinated with and channeled through Iraq's national government.

In a statement released following a May 2015 meeting between President Obama, Vice President Joe Biden, and KRG President Barzani, the White House reiterated the United States' commitment "to a united, federal, and democratic Iraq, as defined in the Iraqi constitution."[108]

APPENDIX. COMPARISON OF PROPOSED FY2016 NATIONAL DEFENSE AUTHORIZATION ACT PROVISIONS AND LEGISLATION TO DIRECTLY ARM CERTAIN IRAQI FORCES

House-enrolled version of the FY2016 NDAA (H.R. 1735)

- The House-enrolled version of the FY2016 NDAA (H.R. 1735) would direct the executive branch to consider the Kurdish *peshmerga*; Sunni tribal security forces with a national security mission; and the Iraqi Sunni National Guard to be eligible for direct security assistance from the United States.
- Section 1223 (d) of H.R. 1735 would amend subsection (j)(1)(B) of Section 1236 of the FY2015 NDAA to state that, "notwithstanding any other provision of law," these entities "shall each be deemed to meet the eligibility requirements of section 3 of the Arms Export Control Act (22 U.S.C. 2753) and chapter 2 of part II of the Foreign Assistance Act of 1961 (22 U.S.C. 2311 et seq.)"

- These provisions of the Arms Export Control Act and the Foreign Assistance Act have long been understood to preclude the direct provision of U.S. security assistance to entities other than the security forces of a country's national government or an international organization, in line with general U.S. foreign policy goals that have sought to promote international respect for the sovereignty of national governments and the unity and territorial integrity of countries receiving U.S. assistance.

- Of the FY2016 OCO funds that would be authorized for Iraq security assistance by the bill, H.R. 1735 would require that "not less than 25 percent" be obligated and expended "for assistance directly to" the entities named in the bill. Of that 25 percent, the House version directs 12.5 percent to the Kurdish *peshmerga*. The House version would exempt the provision of security assistance to named entities from cost-sharing requirements placed on assistance to the national government of Iraq.
- The bill would require the Obama Administration to submit an assessment of the government of Iraq's performance relative to a series of conditions, including whether or not the Iraqi government has adopted legislation creating an Iraqi Sunni National Guard and ensuring the U.S. assistance are "appropriately distributed" to the named forces.
- Should the Administration fail to submit the assessment or make adverse findings about the government of Iraq's performance, the bill would require that assistance to the government of Iraq be withheld until the conditions are met and that an additional 60 percent of all unobligated FY2016 funds be directly provided to named forces.

Senate Armed Services Committee(SASC)-reported version of the FY2016 NDAA (S. 1376)

- The SASC reported version of the FY2016 NDAA (S. 1376) does not include new requirements or directions regarding the provision of U.S. assistance directly to individual security forces in Iraq. However, the bill would prohibit the provision of further assistance to Iraq until the Administration certifies that the government of Iraq has taken measures to prevent the transfer of U.S. assistance to extremist groups, including the Islamic State. The bill would require reporting in the event of such transfers and amend broader reporting requirements on assistance to Iraq from a monthly to a quarterly basis.

- The bill also would state the sense of the Senate that the U.S. government should expeditiously supply certain defense articles and services directly to the Kurdistan Regional Government forces associated with the government of Iraq, "in coordination with coalition partners."

House Appropriations Defense Subcommittee Draft of the FY2016 Defense Appropriations Act

- The draft bill would provide $600 million for the Syria train and equip program, prohibit the use of funds for the transfer of man-portable air defense weapons, and authorize the acceptance of foreign contributions and the provision of assistance to third-party governments using the fund.
- The draft bill would appropriate $715 million for the Iraq train and equip program, subject to vetting
- requirements and foreign and Iraqi financial contribution requirements that may be waived for national security reasons.

Other Legislation to Authorize Direct U.S. Assistance to the Kurdistan Regional Government

Legislation in the House (H.R. 1654) and Senate (S. 1188) would specifically authorize the provision of direct security assistance to the Kurdistan Regional Government, subject to different conditions.

- H.R. 1654 states that the President should consult with the government of Iraq in carrying out the three-year authority the bill would create for the President "to provide defense articles, defense services, and related training directly to the Kurdistan Regional Government for the purpose of supporting international coalition efforts against the Islamic State in Iraq and the Levant (ISIL) or any successor group." The bill names specific types of eligible defense articles and services; specifies usage restrictions; and would create reporting mechanisms for Congress to conduct oversight of the use of the new authority.
  The bill states the President "should" notify the Iraqi government prior to providing assistance authorized under the bill.

- S. 1188 would authorize the President for three years to provide—"in consultation with" the Iraqi government—defense articles, defense services, and related training "directly to Kurdistan Regional Government military and security forces associated with the Government of Iraq" for anti-IS efforts. S.1188 identifies as eligible the same defense articles and services as H.1654, and includes the same reference to "other military assistance that the President determines to be appropriate." In excepting authorized assistance from any U.S. legal requirement that recipients of U.S. assistance be a "country or international organization," the bill states that its terms shall not "be construed as establishing a precedent for the future provision of assistance ... to organizations other than a country or international organization." The bill specifies end-use and re-transfer restrictions and would create reporting mechanisms for congressional oversight. The bill states the President "should" notify the Iraqi government prior to providing authorized assistance.

End Notes

[1] Testimony of Secretary Carter and Gen. Dempsey before Senate Foreign Relations Committee, March 11, 2015; Testimony of US CENTCOM Commander General Lloyd Austin before the House Armed Services Committee, March 3, 2015.

[2] Mr. Nicholas J. Rasmussen Acting Director, National Counterterrorism Center, Statement for the Record, Senate Select Intelligence Committee, November 20, 2014.

[3] Background Briefing on Iraq by Senior State Department Official, Washington, DC, May 20, 2015.

[4] In July 2012, Baghdadi warned U.S. leaders that "the mujahidin have set out to chase the affiliates of your armies that have fled.... You will see them in your own country, God willing. The war with you has just begun." U.S. Government Open Source Center (OSC) Report GMP20120721586002, "Islamic State of Iraq Amir Calls on Sunni Tribes to 'Repent,'" July 21, 2012. In 2015, IS Spokesman Adnani urged the group's supporters "in Europe and the disbelieving West and everywhere else, to target the crusaders in their own lands and wherever they are found." OSC Report TRR2015012657315008, "ISIL Spokesman Al-Adnani Announces 'Wilayah Khurasan,' Calls For More Lone Wolf Attacks in West," Twitter, January 26, 2015.

[5] OSC Report TRR2014111361251279, "ISIL Amir Al-Baghdadi Accepts Pledges of Allegiance, Announces 'Expansion' to Saudi Arabia, Yemen," Twitter, November 13, 2014.

[6] OSC Report TRN2014051234500562, "Al-Furqan Releases ISIL Al-Adnani's Message Criticizing Al-Zawahiri, Refusing to Leave Syria," Twitter, May 11-12, 2014.

[7] AP, "Syria's Assad: Turkey played key role in fall of city of Idlib to Islamic fighters," April 17, 2015.

[8] OSC Report LIN2015050430405051, "Syrian Opposition Sources Cited on Efforts in Istanbul To 'Unify' Armed 'Islamic' Factions," *Al Hayah* (London), May 4, 2015.

[9] CJCS Dempsey, Remarks at Press Conference with Secretary of Defense Ashton Carter, May 7, 2015.

[10] OSC Report TRL2015042948492010, ISIL Statement Calls on Jihadists in Syria To 'Reinforce Al Anbar and Salah ad Din Fronts' in Iraq," April 28, 2015; and, Kareem Fahimnov, Strikes by U.S. Blunt ISIS but Anger Civilians, *New York Times*, November 13, 2014.

[11] For example, President Obama said in a May 2015 interview with Al Arabiya television that "The problem we also have is that on the other side inside of Syria, we have extremists who may be opposed to Assad but also deeply opposed to the United States, are deeply opposed to the GCC countries; are interested in establishing a very destructive order and have engaged in the same kinds of brutality and violence that we don't want to see deeply entrenched." In March 2015, CIA Director John Brennan said, "None of us, Russia, the United States, coalition, and regional states, wants to see a collapse of the government and political institutions in Damascus. ... I think that's a legitimate concern from the standpoint of what we don't want to do is to allow those extremist elements that in some parts of Syria are ascendant right now. We have ISIL. We have Jabhat al-Nusra, the al-Qaeda element within Syria... And the last thing we want to do is to allow them to march into Damascus. That's why it's important to bolster those forces within the Syrian opposition that are not extremists." Remarks of CIA Director Brennan, "U.S. Intelligence in a Transforming World," Council on Foreign Relations (New York), March 13, 2015.

[12] OSC Report IML2015012330825913, January 23, 2015.

[13] Mousab Alhamadee, "Another Syrian group charges that U.S. airstrikes killed civilians," McClatchy News, May 6, 2015.

[14] "The Islamic State Eyes Expansion in Damascus," Institute for the Study of War, January 21, 2015.

[15] Background Briefing on Iraq by Senior State Department Official, Washington, DC, May 20, 2015.

[16] See, for example, "New Iraq Militias Take a Lead in Tikrit Fight," *Wall Street Journal*, April 1, 2015.

[17] U.S. Government Open Source Center Report LIL2015040372242282, April 3, 2015.

[18] Background Briefing on Iraq by Senior State Department Official, Washington, DC, May 20, 2015.

[19] OSC Report LIN2015040132577415, April 1, 2015.

[20] U.S. to deliver 2,000 anti-tank weapons to Iraq, Pentagon says, May 21, 2015.

[21] Ahmed Ali. "Calm Down. ISIS Isn't Winning." *New York Times*, May 22, 2015.

[22] Brigadier General Thomas D. Weidley (USMC), Chief of Staff, Combined Joint Task Force-Operation Inherent Resolve cited IS fighters use of Iraqi and Kurdish uniforms, changes to their travel patterns, use of IEDs and infrastructure destruction to slow pursuing forces, preparation of defensive positions in Mosul and other areas, and limits on civilian activity. Department of Defense press briefing, May 15, 2015.

[23] Background Briefing on Iraq by Senior State Department Official, Washington, DC, May 20, 2015.

[24] Briefing by White House Spokesman Josh Earnest, May 26, 2015.

[25] Background Briefing on Iraq by Senior State Department Official, Washington, DC, May 20, 2015.

[26] Council on Foreign Relations, Conversation with Iraqi Kurdish President Masoud Barzani, May 8, 2015.

[27] White House Office of the Press Secretary, "Statement by the President on ISIL," September 10, 2014.

[28] The website of the Special Presidential Envoy for the Global Coalition to Counter ISIL identifies five "lines of effort" guiding the coalition's efforts: (1) Providing military support to our partners; (2) Impeding the flow of foreign fighters; (3) Stopping ISIL's financing and funding; (4) Addressing humanitarian crises in the region; and (5) Exposing ISIL's true nature.

[29] White House Office of the Press Secretary, "Statement by the President on ISIL," September 10, 2014.

[30] *Reuters*, "Assad seeks agreement over U.S. air strikes in Syria," January 26, 2015.

[31] See for example, Dov Zakheim, "The Only ISIS Strategy Left for America: Containment," *The National Interest*, May 23, 2015.

[32] Micah Zenko, "Nine Months of Coalition Air Strikes Against the Islamic State," Council on Foreign Relations, May 8, 2015.

[33] According to the Defense Intelligence Agency, "The Khorasan Group is a cadre of experienced al-Qa'ida operatives that works closely with and relies upon al-Nusrah Front to provide personnel and space for training facilities in northwestern Syria. The group is primarily focused on transnational terrorist attack plotting. Coalition airstrikes in Syria probably killed a number of senior al-Nusrah Front and Khorasan Group operatives, but the group almost certainly has maintained some capability to continue plotting against Western interests." Joint Statement, House Armed Services Committee, February 3, 2015.

[34] For example, see testimony of Chairman of the Joint Chiefs of Staff General Martin Dempsey, Senate Armed Services Committee. "Hearing on the U.S. Policy Towards Iraq, Syria, and ISIL," September 14, 2014.

[35] Testimony of U.S. Air Force Lt. Gen. Ellen M. Pawlikowski and Lt. Gen. James M. Holmes, House Armed Services Committee Subcommittee on Tactical Air and Land Forces, March 26, 2015.

[36] Briefing by White House Spokesman Josh Earnest, May 26, 2015.

[37] In December 2014, the Department of Defense authorized the deployment of 1,000 members of the Third Brigade Combat Team, 82nd Airborne Division from Fort Bragg, NC, along with 300 enabling personnel drawn from various Army, Air Force, and Marine Corps units. DOD Press Briefing by Rear Admiral John Kirby, January 6, 2014; and, Paul McLeary, "U.S. troops under mortar fire in Iraq," January 5, 2015.

[38] Statement by the White House Press Secretary on Additional U.S. Steps in the Counter-ISIL Effort, June 10, 2015.

[39] The five locations are Al Asad, Erbil, Baghdad, Taji and Besmayah. Michelle Tan, "Inside the Iraq mission: What our troops are doing," *ArmyTimes*, April 3, 2015.

[40] The White House Office of the Press Secretary, FACT SHEET: U.S.-Iraq Cooperation, April 14, 2015.

[41] Eric Schmitt and Michael Gordon, "U.S. Sees Risks in Assisting a Compromised Iraqi Force," *New York Times*, July 14, 2014.

[42] Gen. Dempsey told the House Armed Services Committee on November 13, "I'm not predicting, at this point, that I would recommend that those [Iraqi] forces in Mosul and along the border would need to be accompanied by U.S. forces, but we're certainly considering it."

[43] U.S. Defense Security Cooperation Agency (DSCA), Transmittal No: 14-33, July 29, 2014. In April 2015, U.S. officials reported that 1,700 HELLFIRE missiles had been delivered.

[44] The White House, Office of the Press Secretary, FACT SHEET: U.S.-Iraq Cooperation, April 14, 2015.

[45] DSCA, Transmittal No: 11-46, December 12, 2011.

[46] U.S. Army, Security assistance enterprise delivers vehicles to Iraq, January 28, 2015.

[47] DSCA, Transmittal No: 14-34, December 19, 2014; and, Transmittal No: 14-45, December 19, 2014.

[48] DSCA, Transmittal No: 13-18 and Transmittal No. 13-29, January 27, 2014.

[49] U.S. to deliver 2,000 anti-tank weapons to Iraq, Pentagon says, May 21, 2015.

[50] According to the defense authorizing committee leaders who drafted the bill, their version of the authorization was amended to specifically: add local security forces with a national security mission to the list of forces authorized to receive assistance under this section. We believe that, for purposes of this section, local security forces should include local forces that are committed to protecting highly vulnerable ethnic and religious minority communities in the Nineveh Plain and elsewhere from the ISIL threat.

[51] In August 2014, press reports suggested the Obama Administration had begun supplying mostly lighter weaponry and ammunition directly to the security forces (*peshmerga*) of the Kurdistan Regional Government (KRG), through intelligence channels. Craig Whitlock and Greg Jaffe, "U.S. Directly Arms Kurdish Forces," *Washington Post*, August 12, 2014. The *peshmerga*, with U.S. assistance, also have retransferred some weapons and ammunition to Syrian Kurdish forces battling Islamic State fighters in Syria. U.S. Central Command news release. "U.S. Resupplies Kurdish Forces Fighting ISIL Near Kobani." October 20, 2014.

[52] Tim Arango. "Iraq Government Reaches Accord with the Kurds." *New York Times*, December 3, 2014; and, Deb Riechmann, "Kurdish leader reiterates his forces need for arms," Associated Press, May 8, 2015.

[53] The White House, Office of the Press Secretary, FACT SHEET: U.S.-Iraq Cooperation, April 14, 2015.

[54] In remarks at the Council on Foreign Relations on May 8, 2015, President Barzani said "we have been given assurances that the *peshmergas* will get the weapons and the requirements into their hands." CQ Transcript, Council on Foreign Relations Holds Conversation With Iraqi Kurdish President Masoud Barzani.

[55] Background Briefing on Iraq by Senior State Department Official, Washington, DC, May 20, 2015.

[56] Nour Malas, "Iraq Begins Training of Sunni Tribal Fighters to Stem Advance of Islamic State," *Wall Street Journal*, May 10, 2015; and, and *As Sabah al Jadeed* (The New Morning, Iraq), "First Training Center Opens for Fighters from the Clans of Amiriyat al Fallujah," May 10, 2015.

[57] Ibid.

[58] Background Briefing on Iraq by Senior State Department Official, Washington, DC, May 20, 2015.

[59] According to Iraq's Khabar News, Kurdish MP Shakhwan Abdallah said that "some Iraqi components do not want the formations of the national guard to be directly connected with the commander in chief of the Armed Forces. They want the governors to assume the responsibility of leading those formations. They also want those formations to be better-equipped than the police but not as good-equipped as the Army." OSC Report LIL2015052368195952, May 23, 2015.

[60] Hamza Mustafa, "Iraqi parliament rejects US bill to 'split Iraq,'" *Al Sharq Al Awsat* (London), May 3, 2015; and Michael R. Gordon, "2 Sunni Leaders Denounce Lack of Role in Iraqi Government," *New York Times*, Mat 11, 2015.

[61] For more on this program and related legislation, see CRS Report R43727, *Train and Equip Authorities for Syria: In Brief*, by Christopher M. Blanchard and Amy Belasco. The FY2015 continuing resolution (H.J.Res. 124, P.L. 113-164) authorizes the Department of Defense through December 11, 2014, or until the passage of a FY2015 defense authorization act to provide overt assistance, including training, equipment, supplies, and sustainment, to vetted members of the Syrian opposition and other vetted Syrians for select purposes. Congress amended and extended this authority in the FY2015 NDAA (Section 1209 of P.L. 113-291) and FY2015 appropriations act (Section 9016 of P.L. 113-235). The NDAA and its accompanying explanatory statement further specify the types of assistance to be provided, and expand reporting requirements, include human rights and rule of law commitment vetting requirements, authorize the provision of assistance to third countries for the purposes of the program, and create a broad waiver authority for the President relative to the assistance program, subject to a 30-day congressional notification period.

[62] Dasha Afanasieva, Warren Strobel and Phil Stewart, "Set to begin, U.S. plan for Syrian rebels already mired in doubt," Reuters, April 27, 2015; and, W.J. Hennigan and Patrick J. McDonnell, "$500-million program to train anti-Islamic State fighters appears stalled," Los Angeles Times, May 4, 2015.

[63] Briefing by Secretary of Defense Ashton Carter and CJCS General Martin E. Dempsey, May 7, 2015.

[64] Ibid; and, Testimony of Secretary Carter and Gen. Dempsey before Senate Foreign Relations Committee, March 11. 2015.

[65] For more information, see CRS Report R43980, *Islamic State Financing and U.S. Policy Approaches*, by Carla E. Humud, Robert Pirog, and Liana W. Rosen.

[66] Under Secretary of the Treasury for Terrorism and Financial Intelligence David Cohen, Remarks at the Carnegie Endowment for International Peace, October 23, 2014.

[67] "Terrorist Financing and the Islamic State," testimony submitted by Matthew Levitt to the House Committee on Financial Services, November 13, 2014.

[68] House Financial Services Committee hearing on Terrorist Financing and the Islamic State, November 13, 2014.

[69] Remarks by Secretary of State John Kerry at a joint press conference with U.K. Foreign Secretary Hammond and Iraqi Prime Minister Abadi, January 22, 2015.

[70] "Islamic State group sets out first budget, worth $2bn," *Al Araby al Jadeed*, January 4, 2015.

[71] U.S. Treasury Department, Treasury Designates Twelve Foreign Terrorist Fighter Facilitators, September 24, 2014.

[72] House Financial Services Committee hearing on Terrorist Financing and the Islamic State, November 13, 2014.

[73] See White House, Fact Sheet: Comprehensive U.S. Government Approach to Foreign Terrorist Fighters in Syria and the Broader Region, September 24, 2014.

[74] Mr. Nicholas J. Rasmussen Acting Director, National Counterterrorism Center, Statement for the Record, Senate Select Intelligence Committee, November 20, 2014. In September 2014, his predecessor Matthew Olsen had said that "we have no credible information that ISIL is planning to attack the U.S.". Olsen also said U.S. counterterrorism officials "remain mindful of the possibility that an ISIL-sympathizer—perhaps motivated by online propaganda—could conduct a limited, self-directed attack here at home with no warning."

However, Olsen noted that, "In our view, any threat to the U.S. homeland from these types of extremists is likely to be limited in scope and scale."

[75] On February 11, U.S. National Counterterrorism Director Nicholas Rasmussen said, "The rate of foreign fighter travel to Syria is unprecedented. It exceeds the rate of travelers who went to Afghanistan and Pakistan, Iraq, Yemen, or Somalia at any point in the last 20 years." Statement of Nicholas J. Rasmussen, Director, U.S. National Counterterrorism Center, before the House Committee on Homeland Security, February 11, 2015.

[76] Background Briefing on Iraq by Senior State Department Official, Washington, DC, May 20, 2015

[77] Ibid.

[78] In Iraq, U.S.-led airstrikes halted the Islamic State advance on Irbil and enabled the Kurdish *peshmerga* and Iraqi Security Forces (ISF) to safely evacuate most of the Yazidi internally displaced persons (IDPs) from Sinjar Mountain. Additional strikes helped *peshmerga* and ISF forces drive Islamic State fighters from Mosul Dam, which the Islamic State purportedly could have used to flood large parts of Iraq. In September, U.S. airstrikes facilitated efforts by the ISF and Shiite militias to break an Islamic State siege of the Shiite Turkmen-inhabited town of Amerli. DOD News release, "Obama Praises Success of Humanitarian Operations in Iraq," August 14, 2014.

[79] Testimony of US CENTCOM Commander General Lloyd Austin before the House Armed Services Committee, March 3, 2015.

[80] Remarks by President Obama and Prime Minister Al Abadi of Iraq after Bilateral Meeting, April 14, 2015.

[81] For more information, see CRS Report R43760, *A New Authorization for Use of Military Force Against the Islamic State: Issues and Current Proposals in Brief.*

[82] Available at http://www.cq.com/doc/4622425?0&pos=alert&dlvid=115410051&agenttype=13.

[83] President Barack Obama, Letter from the President—Authorization for the Use of United States Armed Forces in connection with the Islamic State of Iraq and the Levant, February 11, 2015, http://www.whitehouse.gov/the-pressoffice/2015/02/11/letter-president-authorization-use-united-states-armed-forces-connection.

[84] Susanne Koelbl, "Interview with Iraqi Prime Minister Al-Abadi: 'The Liberation of Tikrit Is Very Encouraging,'" *Spiegel* (Hamburg), April 3, 2015.

[85] Readout of the President and Vice President's Meeting with Iraqi KRG President Masoud Barzani, May 5, 2015.

[86] Department of Defense, Remarks by Secretary Carter to Troops in Fort Drum, New York, March 30, 2015.

[87] Akbar Shahid Ahmed, Kurdish Leader Aligns with White House over Congress on ISIS Strategy, Huffington Post, May 7, 2015.

[88] White House Office of the Press Secretary. Press Briefing by Josh Earnest. May 19, 2015.

[89] Maeve Reston, "GOP grapples with ground troops in Iraq," CNN, May 21, 2015.

[90] Gen. Dempsey told the House Armed Services Committee on November 13, "I'm not predicting, at this point, that I would recommend that those [Iraqi] forces in Mosul and along the border would need to be accompanied by U.S. forces, but we're certainly considering it."

[91] Text of White House's Formal War Authorization Proposal. February 11, 2015.

[92] Tim Arango. "Key Iraqi City Falls to ISIS as Last of Security Forces Flee." *New York Times*, May 17, 2015.

[93] The President said, "our attitude towards Asad continues to be that you know, through his actions, through using chemical weapons on his own people, dropping barrel bombs that

killed innocent children that he—he has foregone legitimacy. But when it comes to our policy and the coalition that we're putting together, our focus specifically is on ISIL. It’s narrowly on ISIL.” President Obama interview with NBC News Meet the Press, September 6, 2014.

[94] Readout of Special Envoy Rubinstein's Travel to Moscow, State Department Media Note, May 18, 2015.

[95] Testimony of Secretary of State John Kerry, Secretary of Defense Ashton Carter, and Chairman of the Joint Shiefs of Staff General Martin Dempsey before the Senate Foreign Relations Committee. March 11, 2015; and Briefing by Secretary of Defense Ashton Carter and CJCS General Martin E. Dempsey, May 7, 2015.

[96] Babak Dehghanpisheh, “Iran Dramatically Shifts Iraq Policy to Confront Islamic State,” Reuters, September 2, 2014.

[97] Ibid.

[98] Jay Solomon and Carol Lee, “Obama Wrote Secret Letter to Iran’s Khamenei About Fighting Islamic State,” *Wall Street Journal*, November 6, 2014.

[99] “Iran News Agency Reports Death of Iranian Pilot in Iraq,” Radio Free Europe/Radio Liberty, July 5, 2014.

[100] Some direct deliveries to these forces reportedly have been approved by the Baghdad government.

[101] See for example, the references to “country or international organization” in the Arms Export Control Act’s section on eligibility for defense articles and defense services (22 U.S.C. § 2753) and in the Foreign Assistance Act of 1961’s sections on security assistance(22 U.S.C. § 2301 et seq). The Defense Security Cooperation Agency’s Security Assistance Management Manual states that “Defense articles and services are not generally sold to foreign purchasers under the AECA unless they are part of the national defense establishment, under the direction and control of the ministry responsible for defense matters.” See Chapter 4, available at http://www.samm.dsca.mil/chapter/chapter-4.

[102] Daniel DePetris, “2016 National Defense Authorization Act: 4 Big Takeaways,” The National Interest, May 13, 2015.

[103] Available at http://pmo.iq/pme/press2015en/29-4-20151en.htm. Arabic statement available at http://pmo.iq/press2015/29-4-20151.htm.

[104] Statement, April 30, 2015. Available at http://www.mofa.gov.iq/en/news/statement-20150430094615. Arabic statement available at http://www.mofa.gov.iq/news/by-n-20150429065425.

[105] Hamza Mustafa, “Iraqi parliament rejects US bill to ‘split Iraq,’” *Al Sharq Al Awsat* (London), May 3, 2015.

[106] *Al Ghad* Press (Iraq), “Sadr: New U.S. Draft Bill is the Beginning of the Division of Iraq,” April 29, 2015.

[107] U.S. Government Open Source Center (OSC) Report TRN2015042957931297, “Iraq: Imam Ali Brigades Accuses US of 'Plot to Partition Iraq',” April 29, 2015.

[108] Readout of the President and Vice President’s Meeting with Iraqi KRG President Masoud Barzani, May 5, 2015.

INDEX

#

9/11, 2, 59

A

access, 88
Afghanistan, 12, 19, 37, 38, 39, 40, 41, 43, 44, 45, 46, 47, 53, 57, 63, 90, 93, 116
Africa, 39
agencies, 89
aggression, 42
Air Force, 113
Al Qaeda, vii, 1, 2, 3, 11, 12, 16, 19, 20, 37, 38, 39, 40, 41, 42, 43, 44, 45, 46, 47, 48, 49, 56, 65, 72, 80, 88, 89, 90, 92, 94, 97, 98, 100
Algeria, 12
al-Zarqawi, Abu Musab, 65
appropriations, 62, 82, 85, 86, 87, 103, 105, 106, 115
Appropriations Act, 108
Arabian Peninsula, 45
armed conflict, 5, 37, 39, 43, 46
armed forces, 77
armed groups, 90
arrest(s), 53, 72
assault, 72, 74, 76
assessment, 81, 108
assets, 62
atrocities, 100
Attorney General, 58
authorities, 5, 16, 20, 43, 45, 47, 50, 55, 56, 62, 84, 85, 88, 94, 103, 106, 107
autonomy, 97

B

Bahrain, 89
ban, 18
banks, 71, 88
base, 38, 81, 85
Biden, Vice President Joseph, 108
bilateral, 19, 40, 46, 102
border crossing, 70, 74
breakdown, 15
breathing, 4
brothers, 75
brutality, 112
Bush, President, 19, 38, 41, 57
Bush, President George Walker, 38, 41, 57

C

campaigns, 12, 104
capacity building, 81
certification, 11, 16, 34, 35, 87
chain of command, 96
challenges, 15, 47, 72, 75, 89, 95, 96, 103
chemical, 100, 116

Chief of Staff, 112
children, 117
CIA, 112
cities, 61, 96
citizens, 4, 19, 27, 44, 51, 54, 62, 90
civil war, 61, 62, 63, 70, 86, 101
CNN, 116
communities, 94, 95, 114
community, 17, 55, 63, 89, 97
competing interests, 12
conference, 36, 115
conflict, 9, 12, 19, 39, 43, 46, 48, 63, 64, 71, 78, 90, 99, 100, 101, 105
conformity, 52
confrontation, 64
congress, 59
consensus, 21
Constitution, 2, 4, 37, 39, 47, 52, 53
contradiction, 92
controversial, 4, 51
cooperation, 11, 18, 19, 23, 29, 43, 78, 93, 102
coordination, 18, 22, 43, 70, 77, 82, 83, 95, 97, 108
cost, 82, 105, 108
Council of Ministers, 74
counterterrorism, 16, 37, 38, 39, 40, 43, 45, 46, 48, 49, 52, 53, 59, 115
counterterrorism strategy, 37, 39
creep, 59
criticism, 51, 62, 74
cruise missiles, 80
Cuba, 45, 57

D

deaths, 64
decentralization, 75
degradation, 100
Department of Defense, 36, 52, 57, 58, 76, 103, 112, 113, 115, 116
Department of the Treasury, 79, 89
deployments, vii, 1, 2, 3, 18, 44, 45, 47, 57, 81
deposits, 89
destruction, 64, 112
detainees, 65
detention, 51, 58
devolution, 95, 99
donations, 88
draft, 2, 7, 40, 44, 86, 92, 108
drawing, 63
due process, 51, 55

E

economic development, 53
Egypt, 12, 63
embassy, 4
employment, 51
enemies, 63, 64
enemy combatants, 51, 52
enforcement, 91
equipment, 23, 62, 82, 83, 89, 101, 106, 115
ethnic groups, 107
Europe, 63, 89, 111, 117
evidence, 75, 77
evolution, 40
execution, 8
executive branch, 3, 19, 38, 39, 42, 43, 45, 46, 48, 49, 55, 56, 104, 106, 108
exercise, 5, 55, 97
expenditures, 20, 32
extremists, 65, 79, 99, 100, 112, 116

F

facilitators, 88
fear(s), 95, 96, 97, 101
Federal Register, 57
feelings, 65
fights, 2
financial, 62, 64, 78, 88, 89, 108
financial community, 88
financial resources, 62, 78, 88
financial system, 88, 89
flexibility, 5, 9, 10, 54, 98
food, 70
foreign affairs, 4

foreign assistance, 6
foreign policy, 4, 108
France, 84
funding, 48, 78, 82, 86, 87, 88, 103, 105, 106, 113
funds, 9, 55, 58, 62, 79, 82, 88, 89, 103, 104, 108

G

gangs, 74
Georgia, 57
Germany, 84
God, 111
governance, 38
governments, 51, 87, 106, 108
growth, 99
Guantanamo, 45, 51, 52, 57, 58

H

heroism, 74
Hezbollah, 71
homeland security, 61, 64, 89
homes, 73
host, 87, 103
hostilities, 7, 21, 45, 92
hotspots, 96
House, 14, 34, 36, 41, 42, 82, 85, 87, 92, 101, 104, 105, 106, 107, 108, 111, 113, 115, 116
House of Representatives, 41, 42
human, 6, 17, 25, 115
human right(s), 6, 17, 25, 115
humanitarian crises, 113
Hussein, Saddam, 3, 44, 61

I

IDA, 103, 104
identification, 16, 20, 55
identity, 96
ideology, 16, 25
Immigration and Nationality Act, 59
improvements, 70
income, 88
independence, 84
individuals, 7, 10, 11, 17, 25, 41, 45, 47, 51, 53, 80, 89, 90, 91, 92
infrastructure, 44, 82, 91, 112
institutions, 112
insurgency, 61
integrity, 108
intelligence, vii, 1, 6, 18, 27, 62, 63, 70, 78, 81, 89, 93, 114
intelligence gathering, vii, 1, 78
interference, 108
internally displaced, 103, 116
international law, 17, 25, 43, 46, 52, 53, 54, 90
International Narcotics Control, 103
international terrorism, 41
intervention, 101
Iran, 63, 79, 95, 96, 101, 102, 108, 117
Islam, 72
issues, vii, 6, 10, 15, 36, 40, 51, 58, 84, 92

J

Jews, 64
Jordan, 19, 87, 104
jurisdiction, 33
justification, 4, 49

K

kill, 45, 55
Kurds, 62, 65, 95, 102, 108, 114

L

law enforcement, 53
laws, 88, 91, 106, 107
lead, 8, 73, 79, 93
leadership, 12, 64, 65, 80, 88, 91, 99
Lebanon, 19, 71, 104
Lee, Barbara, 6, 56

legislation, 7, 21, 37, 39, 42, 43, 53, 56, 58, 62, 77, 84, 86, 87, 88, 91, 92, 105, 107, 108, 115
legislative authority, 49
legislative proposals, 21, 38, 40, 55, 58, 84, 95, 106
light, 13, 19, 50, 74
loans, 89
logistics, 82, 95, 106
loyalty, 65

M

majority, 34
manpower, 62, 70, 78
Marine Corps, 113
mass, 72, 83
materials, 63, 64
matter, 11, 35, 55, 86, 107
media, 36, 57, 58, 63, 72, 73, 90, 96
membership, 18
messages, 64
Middle East, 13, 39, 64, 79, 89
military pressure, 100
militia(s), 71, 73, 74, 75, 81, 95, 96, 97, 99, 102, 104, 107, 116
minorities, 62, 80
minority groups, 95
mission, 39, 40, 44, 46, 53, 59, 77, 82, 84, 92, 105, 108, 113, 114
monopoly, 70
morale, 94
Moscow, 99, 117
Muslims, 63

N

National Counterterrorism Center(NCTC), 64, 90, 111, 115, 116
National Defense Authorization Act, 56, 59, 82, 87, 101, 104, 105, 108, 117
national security, 3, 4, 9, 10, 11, 16, 17, 25, 38, 40, 43, 44, 47, 52, 80, 82, 84, 95, 105, 108, 114
nationality, 91
NATO, 18, 23, 44
negotiating, 100
Nigeria, 63, 93
North Africa, 13
nuclear program, 102
nuclear talks, 102

O

Obama Administration, 2, 3, 5, 11, 13, 19, 37, 39, 40, 43, 45, 46, 47, 48, 51, 52, 81, 87, 92, 93, 100, 103, 108, 114
Obama, President Barack, vii, 1, 5, 16, 36, 39, 46, 57, 58, 62, 71, 75, 78, 79, 80, 81, 87, 91, 98, 99, 102, 105, 108, 112, 116, 117
obedience, 65
obstacles, 97
officials, 2, 3, 42, 43, 45, 46, 47, 48, 49, 51, 62, 63, 64, 70, 71, 73, 74, 75, 78, 80, 81, 83, 84, 85, 86, 87, 89, 90, 91, 92, 93, 94, 96, 97, 98, 99, 100, 101, 114, 115
oil, 73, 84, 88, 89
openness, 99
operations, 3, 5, 6, 7, 8, 10, 11, 12, 13, 17, 18, 19, 21, 27, 37, 38, 40, 43, 44, 45, 46, 47, 48, 49, 50, 53, 58, 62, 63, 70, 71, 73, 75, 77, 79, 80, 81, 82, 87, 88, 90, 91, 92, 93, 95, 96, 98, 99, 101, 102, 103
opportunities, 99, 100, 101
OSC, 111, 112, 114, 117
oversight, 38, 40, 49, 51, 85, 108

P

paints, 63
Pakistan, 37, 39, 45, 80, 116
parallel, 70, 86, 101
participants, 87
partition, 108
Pentagon, 112, 114
permission, 64, 78
permit, 91

perpetration, 91
perpetrators, 41, 49, 89
Philippines, 57
pipeline, 83
police, 75, 85, 114
policy, 4, 6, 38, 47, 48, 73, 79, 83, 87, 88, 98, 100, 101, 106, 117
policy initiative, 100
policy options, 87
political legitimacy, 52
political problems, 62, 63, 98
politics, 56, 59
population, 61, 72, 96
Posse Comitatus Act, 52, 58
precedent, 55, 101, 108
precedents,
preparation, 112
preservation, 78
president, 36, 57, 58, 116
presidential authority, 9, 13, 18, 42, 50, 53, 54
prevention, 17, 41
principles, 101
propaganda, 64, 115
protection, 4, 17, 18, 27, 81, 82, 101

R

reading, 57, 86
rebel groups, 44, 72, 94
recommendations, 54, 98
recruiting, 63, 89, 90
reform, 47
refugees, 103
regions of the world, 45
reintroduction, 98
rejection, 107
relief, 103
rendition, 51
repair, 82
replacement ratios, 63
reporters, 70
requirement(s), 6, 8, 13, 24, 40, 45, 48, 51, 52, 85, 87, 89, 105, 108, 114, 115
resistance, 73, 74
resolution, 6, 16, 18, 20, 21, 22, 23, 25, 29, 31, 33, 34, 35, 50, 56, 86, 88, 89, 99, 115
resources, 79, 88, 97
response, 2, 19, 36, 37, 38, 39, 41, 55, 91, 92, 103
restoration, 3, 44
restrictions, 54, 59, 94, 108
revenue, 88
Revolutionary Guard, 102
rights, 17
risk(s), 79, 101
roots, 65
routes, 88
rule of law, 115
rules, 21
Russia, 112

S

sabotage, 74
safe haven(s), 93, 103
sanctions, 88, 89, 90
Saudi Arabia, 12, 63, 87, 111
scope, 9, 10, 13, 15, 17, 21, 38, 39, 40, 41, 42, 43, 45, 48, 50, 51, 53, 77, 97, 100, 116
Secretary of Defense, 82, 85, 96, 112, 115, 117
Secretary of the Treasury, 88, 115
sectarianism, 99
security, vii, 1, 4, 7, 10, 17, 19, 20, 29, 40, 46, 58, 59, 62, 63, 64, 71, 74, 78, 80, 82, 83, 84, 85, 86, 89, 92, 94, 95, 96, 97, 105, 106, 107, 108, 114, 117
security assistance, 82, 84, 97, 105, 106, 108, 117
security forces, vii, 1, 4, 62, 74, 78, 80, 82, 84, 85, 86, 95, 97, 105, 106, 107, 108, 114
security services, 19
security threats, 59
seizure, 70, 72
Senate, 5, 14, 34, 36, 41, 42, 57, 58, 83, 85, 87, 92, 101, 105, 106, 108, 111, 113, 115, 117

Senate Foreign Relations Committee, 5, 14, 111, 115, 117
September 11, 2, 16, 36, 37, 38, 39, 40, 41, 42, 44, 45, 46, 47, 48, 49, 53, 57, 58
services, 29, 82, 108, 117
shape, 10, 49, 50, 95
Shiites, 63, 65, 75
smuggling, 88
society, 107
solution, 86, 92, 99, 100
Somalia, 37, 39, 45, 116
sovereignty, 3, 44, 101, 107, 108
Soviet Union, 90
speculation, 98
speech, vii, 1
stability, 9, 44
stabilization, 101
state(s), 12, 15, 16, 17, 36, 41, 45, 48, 51, 52, 93, 96, 107, 108
state borders, 12
State of the Union address, 2
stretching, 71
structure, 10, 107
suicide, 76
Sunnis, 63, 86, 95, 97, 108
Supreme Court, 57

T

tactics, 3, 17, 47, 62, 63, 76, 77
Taliban, 3, 11, 19, 37, 38, 39, 41, 42, 43, 44, 46, 56, 94
tanks, 83
target, 11, 15, 16, 19, 39, 41, 42, 50, 88, 93, 98, 111
Task Force, 59, 112
technology, 51
tension(s), 65, 75, 77, 91
territorial, 78, 108
territory, 27, 38, 51, 70, 71, 78, 81, 82, 84, 91, 97, 100, 101, 105
terrorism, 25, 38, 41, 42, 48, 51, 52, 54, 55, 100, 101, 104
terrorist acts, 91
terrorist attack(s), 2, 17, 25, 37, 38, 39, 40, 41, 44, 46, 47, 53, 54, 80, 113
terrorist groups, 12, 16, 17, 20, 24, 45, 47, 49, 53, 54, 88, 100
terrorist organization, 59, 90
terrorists, 54, 55, 96, 105
threats, 3, 16, 39, 42, 48, 49, 50, 52, 54, 64, 80, 89, 100, 101, 105
trade, 89
trainees, 101
training, 6, 12, 18, 23, 27, 36, 62, 71, 75, 78, 80, 81, 82, 83, 84, 85, 86, 87, 97, 98, 99, 101, 102, 108, 113, 115
trajectory, 77
transactions, 88
transparency, 49
transport, 88
Treasury, 89, 115
tribesmen, 99
Turkey, 19, 70, 71, 87, 112

U

U.N. Security Council, 6, 18, 20, 22, 35, 88, 89, 90
U.S. assistance, 74, 77, 82, 84, 85, 95, 96, 101, 105, 106, 107, 108, 114
U.S. policy, 38, 44, 62, 78, 83, 84, 94, 95, 102, 106, 107
U.S. Treasury, 115
United Kingdom, 84, 87
United Nations, 3, 6, 31, 44, 88
universe, 10, 11
Unmanned Aerial Vehicles, 51
updating, 54

V

vehicles, 49, 76, 80, 83, 84, 91, 106, 114
Vice President, 108, 116, 117
violence, 17, 25, 63, 112
violent extremist, 16, 25, 83
vision, 63

W

waiver, 115
war, 4, 5, 21, 36, 46, 47, 48, 52, 53, 55, 57, 58, 59, 62, 64, 90, 91, 102, 111
War on Terror, 59
Washington, 59, 73, 77, 83, 84, 96, 111, 112, 114, 116
water, 70
weakness, 91
weapons, 62, 75, 83, 84, 85, 90, 91, 97, 100, 102, 106, 108, 112, 114, 116
White House, 36, 58, 77, 80, 98, 108, 112, 113, 114, 115, 116
withdrawal, 3, 19, 44, 61, 65, 73, 75, 77, 96
WMD, 3
worldview, 63
worldwide, 16

Y

Yemen, 12, 37, 39, 45, 57, 63, 111, 116
yield, 102